Better Homes and Gardens®
STEP-BY-STEP
Deck
Projects

Better Homes and Gardens® Books
Des Moines, Iowa

Better Homes and Gardens® Books
An imprint of Meredith® Books

Step-by-Step Deck Projects
Editors: Benjamin W. Allen, Linda Hallam, Paula Marshall
Associate Art Director: Tom Wegner
Copy Editor: James Sanders
Proofreader: Deborah Morris Smith
Copy Chief: Catherine Hamrick
Copy and Production Editor: Terri Fredrickson
Electronic Production Coordinator: Paula Forest
Editorial and Design Assistants: Jennifer Norris, Karen Schirm, Kaye Chabot, Barbara A. Suk
Production Director: Douglas M. Johnston
Production Manager: Pam Kvitne
Assistant Prepress Manager: Marjorie J. Schenkelberg

Produced by Greenleaf Publishing, Inc.
Publishing Director: Dave Toht
Author: Jeff Beneke
Editor: Steve Cory
Editorial Art Director: Jean DeVaty
Assistant Editor: Rebecca JonMichaels
Design: Melanie Lawson Design
Illustrations: Brian Gilmer, Art Factory

Cover Photograph: Tony Kubat Photography
Production and Back Cover Design: John Seid

Meredith® Books
Editor in Chief: James D. Blume
Design Director: Matt Strelecki
Managing Editor: Gregory H. Kayko
Executive Shelter Editor: Denise L. Caringer

Director, Sales & Marketing, Retail: Michael A. Peterson
Director, Sales & Marketing, Special Markets: Rita McMullen
Director, Sales & Marketing, Home & Garden Center Channel: Ray Wolf
Director, Operations: Valerie Wiese

Vice President, General Manager: Jamie L. Martin

Better Homes and Gardens® Magazine
Editor in Chief: Jean LemMon
Executive Building Editor: Joan McCloskey

Meredith Publishing Group
President, Publishing Group: Christopher Little
Vice President, Consumer Marketing & Development: Hal Oringer

Meredith Corporation
Chairman and Chief Executive Officer: William T. Kerr

Chairman of the Executive Committee: E. T. Meredith III

All of us at Better Homes and Gardens® Books are dedicated to providing you with information and ideas you need to enhance your home. We welcome your comments and suggestions about this book on decks. Write to us at: Better Homes and Gardens® Books, Do-It-Yourself Editorial Department, 1716 Locust St., Des Moines, IA 50309–3023.

Note to the Reader: Due to differing conditions, tools, and individual skills, Meredith Corporation assumes no responsibility for any damages, injuries suffered, or losses incurred as a result of following the information published in this book. Before beginning any project, review the instructions carefully, and if any doubts or questions remain, consult local experts or authorities. Because local codes and regulations vary greatly, you always should check with local authorities to ensure that your project complies with all applicable local codes and regulations. Always read and observe all of the safety precautions provided by any tool or equipment manufacturer, and follow all accepted safety procedures.

TABLE OF CONTENTS

INTRODUCTION

The deck has become an essential feature of many North American homes. Whether for sipping that final cup of coffee on a summer's morning, lounging on a sleepy Sunday afternoon, or throwing together a casual meal for close friends, a deck is the platform of choice for relaxed outdoor living.

Not only is a deck fun to use, it can be fun to build. Most decks can be completed in several weekends without the need for finely tuned carpentry skills. Unlike many remodeling projects, a deck doesn't disrupt your household; the hubbub of construction is safely outdoors.

While decks are fairly straightforward to build, there are many pitfalls to avoid if you are to end up with a well-constructed, long-lasting deck. Perhaps you've heard of decks collapsing because they were not attached properly to houses or were built with framing members that weren't up to the job. Or maybe you've seen how quickly decks can rot if the wrong lumber is used or if members are fastened without concern for moisture defense. Checking a few details as you plan and build your deck will help you avoid such shortcomings.

Step-by-Step Deck Projects explains how outdoor decks are put together, including all the terminology you'll need to speak intelligently to local inspectors and your home center; how to design your own deck; and what fasteners and lumber are required. You'll get step-by-step guidance on each stage of construction. This nuts-and-bolts information is coupled with pockets of inspirational photos that offer plenty of ideas for planning your own deck. The end result will be twofold: an outdoor addition that will help make the summer livin' easy and a selling point that adds value to your home when the time comes to sell it.

Working to Code

Although you may be an amateur working on your own house, you have the same responsibilities as a licensed contractor to meet the legal requirements of your community. Any structure you build must be solid and long-lasting, square and straight, and constructed of materials appropriate to the job. That means using only those techniques and materials that are acceptable to the building codes in your area.

The procedures in this book satisfy most local codes, but be aware that codes vary widely from area to area. Always check with your local building department before beginning a deck project.

Building codes may seem bothersome, but they are designed to make your home safe and worry-free. Ignoring codes can lead to costly mistakes, health hazards, and even difficulties in selling your house. Minor repairs do not require permits. But changes involving framing that improves access to your outdoor living space and major projects, such as a deck, typically require permits. If in doubt, check with your building department before proceeding.

Working With Your Local Building Department

Always make arrangements with your building department before you begin building. Neglecting to do so could cause you the expense and trouble of tearing out and redoing your work.

There's no telling what kind of building inspector you'll get: He or she could be helpful, friendly, and flexible; or you might get a real stickler. No matter what sort of personality you'll be dealing with, your work will go better if you follow these guidelines:

■ This book is a good place to start, but learn as much as you can about each project before you talk with an inspector from your local building department. Then you'll be able to avoid miscommunication and get your permits more quickly. Your building department may have literature concerning your type of installation.

■ Go to your building department with a plan to be approved or amended; don't expect the building department's inspectors to plan the job for you. Present your plan with neatly drawn diagrams and a complete list of the materials you will be using.

■ Be sure you clearly understand when you need to have inspections. Do not cover up work that needs to be inspected.

■ Be as courteous as possible. Inspectors often are wary of homeowners. Show the inspector you are serious about doing things the right way, and comply with any requirements put forth.

How to Use This Book

*S*tep-by-Step Deck Projects* is organized to lead you from deck design and planning straight through to the final details of construction. In the chapters about "Planning a Deck" and "Deck Variations," you will find idea-filled color photos to help you formulate your own deck design. Once you've decided on the type of deck you want to build, review the "Tools and Materials" section and then draw your plans following the guidelines on page 34. The rest of the "Building a Basic Deck" section takes you through the building of a basic 12×20-foot deck. With some adaptation, the steps should apply to your deck design. Variations on this basic theme can be found in the two chapters "Upgrades for the Basic Deck" and "Deck Variations." The final chapter offers finish options and tips on maintenance.

Feature Boxes

*I*n addition to basic instructions, you'll find plenty of tips throughout the book. A "You'll Need" box tells you how long a given task or project will take, what skills are necessary, and what tools you must have. The other tip boxes shown on this page provide practical help to ensure that building your deck will be as pleasurable as possible and will result in a long-lasting and valuable improvement to your home.

CAUTION!
When a how-to step requires special care, Caution! warns you what to watch out for. It will help keep you from doing damage to yourself or the job at hand.

TOOLS TO USE

If you'll need special tools not commonly found in a home-owner's toolbox, we'll tell you about them in Tools to Use.

Money $ Saver

Throwing money at a job does not necessarily make it a better one. Money Saver offers smart ways to accurately estimate your material needs and make wise purchases.

MEASUREMENTS

Keep an eye out for this box when standard measurements or special measuring techniques are called for.

EXPERTS' INSIGHT

Tricks of the trade can make all the difference in helping you do a job quickly and well. Experts' Insight provides insiders' tips on how to make the job easier.

UNDERSTANDING DECK TERMINOLOGY

At first glance, a deck looks like a simple tablelike structure. In fact, decks are comprised of layers of construction, each with its own name and specific function. By taking the time to learn the anatomy of a deck, you will be well on your way to understanding the steps required to construct one. The illustration *below* and the following text identify all of the important components of a typical deck. Specific types of decks may differ a bit; such variations are discussed later in the book.

A deck's foundation provides the critical base of the entire structure and ties it to the earth. The exact size and composition of the foundation depends on your climate, the size of the deck, and other considerations, but it normally consists of **concrete piers.** The foundation must be stationary and strong enough to transfer the load on the deck safely to the ground.

Posts are used on all but the shortest decks. They establish the height of the finished structure. Most decks are built with 4×4 posts. The posts can be cut off below the deck surface or may rise above the surface to provide support for the railing or overhead structure. Posts rest on top of concrete piers.

Beams typically are the first horizontal members of the deck, and they usually are the largest members. Beams are attached to the posts. Most decks are connected to houses by a **ledger.** The ledger functions as another beam, connecting the frame of the deck to the solid foundation of the house.

Joists are the series of boards spanning the distance from beam to beam or beam to ledger. Joists are connected to the ledger with joist hangers; they can overlap, or cantilever, the beam. Joists are spaced 16 or 24 inches on center; that is, they are centered on lines marked every 16 or 24 inches.

A **skirt,** or fascia board, hides the edges of the joists.

The surface layer of the deck is called the **decking,** or deck boards. Decking is fastened to the joists with nails or screws.

If the deck is more than 2 feet above the ground, it should have a railing. While railing designs vary, a standard version consists of **rail posts,** which tie it to the deck frame; **balusters,** usually small, vertical pieces that provide the infill; a **top rail** and **bottom rail,** to which the balusters are attached; and a **cap rail,** which sits atop the entire railing.

Stairs are composed of **treads** (the part you step on), which are fastened to **stringers,** which are the boards that span the distance from the deck surface to the ground. **Risers** are the vertical boards that fill in the space between treads. Risers often are not used on deck stairs.

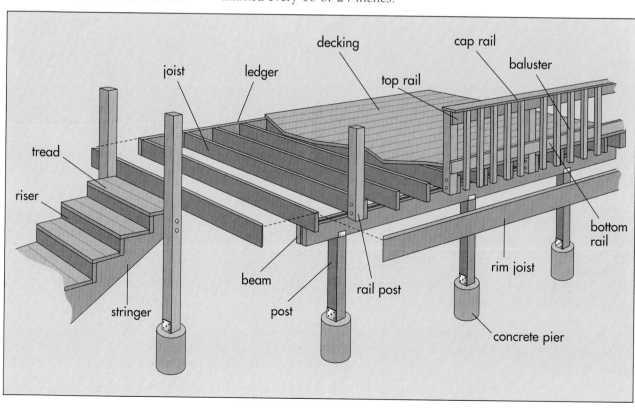

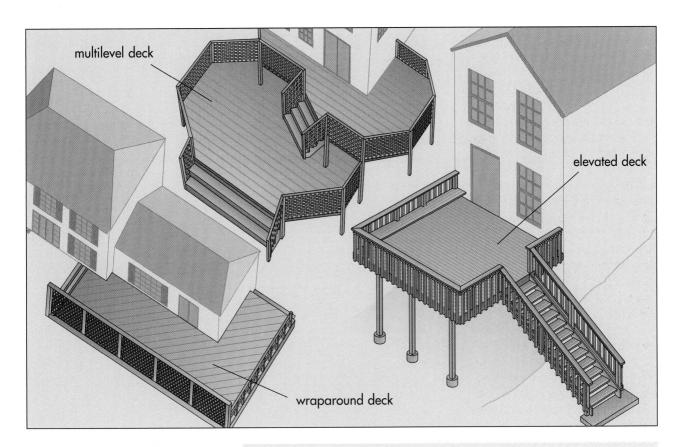

multilevel deck

elevated deck

wraparound deck

Choose a deck configuration.

A well-designed deck should meet your needs and suit the style of your house. Sometimes a simple rectangular deck off the kitchen or family room meets both criteria perfectly. Often, however, circumstances may call for a deck with more drama and variety.

Using the same basic techniques, you can design a deck that wraps around two or more sides of the house. A deck constructed at two or more elevations can be functionally versatile and visually appealing. Decks can serve the ground floor, an upper floor, or both.

A single deck can serve simultaneously as a balcony, porch, stairway, patio, and walkway. And remember, a deck doesn't have to be connected to the house at all; it can stand alone. Budget limitations and construction requirements may limit your dreams, but don't let them stand in the way of a creative design that could solve other problems as well.

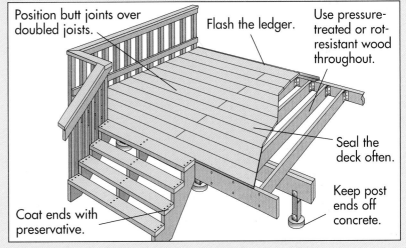

AVOIDING ROT AND WATER DAMAGE

Position butt joints over doubled joists.

Flash the ledger.

Use pressure-treated or rot-resistant wood throughout.

Seal the deck often.

Keep post ends off concrete.

Coat ends with preservative.

Rot-producing fungus is the biggest enemy of wooden decks. To thrive, the fungus requires permanently moist wood. Here are tips on moisture defense:

■ Set posts in metal brackets, away from contact with concrete.

■ A built-up beam (a beam using two separate boards) lasts longer if you use moisture-draining spacers (see page 47).

■ Use butt joints in the decking so water can drain. Position the joints over doubled joists, with spacers between the joists to provide a path for water.

■ Pay careful attention to flashing around the ledger.

■ Brush extra preservative on all cut ends of pressure-treated lumber, especially those surfaces that are horizontal, such as post ends.

CHOOSING A SITE

The best site for your deck may seem obvious, but give the site some careful thought before you plunge in. A deck most often is a transitional structure between your house's interior and exterior. The site you have in mind might solve one problem, only to create another. It can affect traffic patterns through the house and in the yard. The correct site makes such movement seem natural and unobtrusive. A poorly chosen site, however, can block an enjoyable view from inside the house. Or it could unintentionally congregate people near a child's room where you want quiet or a bathroom where you would prefer privacy. A site that is too sunny or too shady may result in an underused deck. Take time as you pick the site to write down your thoughts. List your preferences and draw a site plan to help evaluate the tradeoffs.

EXPERTS' INSIGHT

DECKS AND LANDSCAPING

A deck changes the look of your house and your yard. Most people want to soften the presence of the deck as much as possible. One good way to do that is with a thoughtful landscaping plan. A border garden of perennials, for example, relieves the transition from yard to deck, while shrubs can help camouflage the framing beneath the deck surface. Be sure to keep plantings trimmed so they are not in contact with the deck.

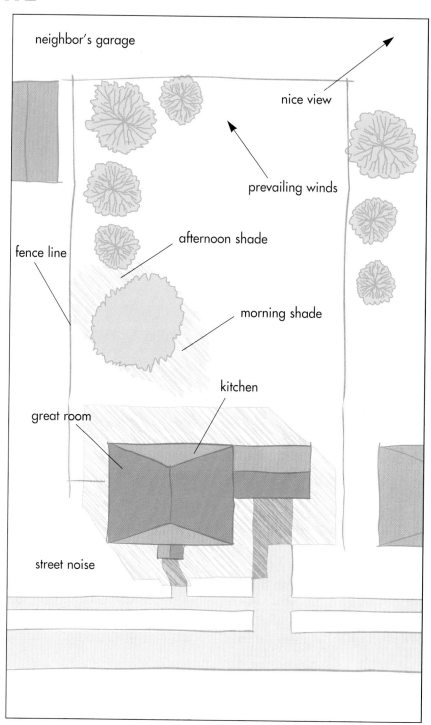

Draw a site plan.
Draw a site plan of your house and yard. Include all doors and windows, as well as utility hookups, walkways, shrubs and trees, and views that you wish to maintain or block out. Note the movement of the sun and how it affects shading and sunlight; be sure to account for seasonal changes. Add every detail that could affect the deck location, such as prevailing winds, buried septic tanks and utility lines, setback requirements, and downspouts. Use tracing paper over the site plan to sketch possible shapes and locations.

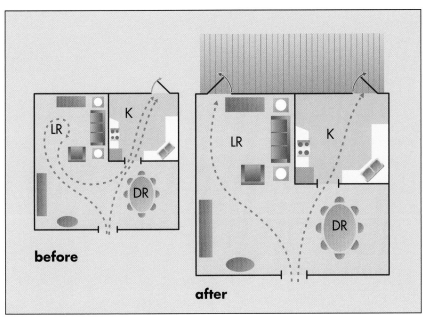

Use a deck to control traffic.
Sometimes a little remodeling can provide the best access to your deck. By adding a door, as shown here, some traffic to the deck is routed through the living room so work in the kitchen isn't interrupted. Retaining the door from the kitchen to the deck allows food and dishes to be carried back and forth with little interference. Conversely, an existing door may be a hindrance to the deck, in which case you may want to consider removing it or replacing it with a window.

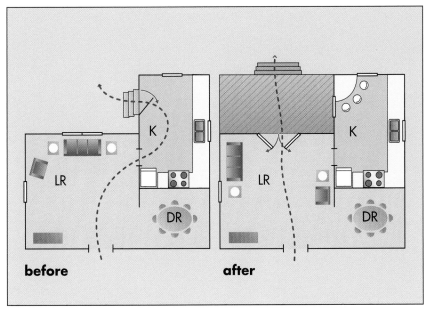

Relocate a doorway.
In this example, moving the back door redirected traffic and significantly improved the kitchen space. A double window in the family room was replaced with a patio door so traffic to the deck and yard was routed away from the kitchen. Replacing the door in the kitchen with a window allowed room for a bright eating area, or the space could have been used for cabinet and counter storage. If the kitchen is large enough, you could also keep the existing door in place.

DETERMINING DECK SIZE AND FUNCTION

If you design your deck for multiple uses, such as a play area for the kids, space for dining, and an area for sunning, it may be tempting to make it as big as possible. It's usually wise to go with the high end of your size estimates—adding more square footage isn't terribly expensive and you want to avoid a cramped deck. But multiple functions don't necessarily require a lot more deck. Sometimes a small design element, such as a level change, can isolate functional zones better than merely adding space to the same single-level deck. If your dreams are big but your budget is tight, plan a deck that can be built in phases.

The decks on these pages show how multiple functions can be combined into decks, both large and small. Each successfully melds with the house and yard to enhance the property while combining multiple functions.

Money $ Saver

HOW BIG?

What is the largest number of people likely to occupy your deck at a given time? A reasonable rule of thumb for planning the size of a deck is to allow 20 square feet of deck area per person. Thus, even a 12×20-foot deck can handle 12 people at once (12x20=240, 240/20=12). More space will be needed, however, if the deck also has tables, chairs, planters, or a grill. If you will have a lot of outdoor furniture on your deck, be sure to test the space with a trial run before building (see page 19).

ABOVE: *Size and function blend gracefully with the simple outlines of this house. The deck's presence is almost camouflaged in the yard-to-house transition, while retaining its usefulness.*

RIGHT: *The ambitious presence of this multilevel deck with its peaked sun screen offers multiple functions, with covered and open areas on top, a dramatic yet gradual stairway between levels, and ample storage underneath.*

This small deck was built with a relatively simple mission: an outdoor foyer. Yet it is nonetheless far from boring. The modest trellis creates the foyer while adding a bit of privacy to the indoors. A basic perimeter bench adds a solidity to the deck edge while providing seating for people and plants alike.

Although it is relatively compact, this project easily handles a variety of functions. The deck was built in stages, as time and money allowed. When rain or insects force most deck dwellers indoors, these homeowners can retreat to the shelter and privacy of the screened porch. The porch is, in fact, a converted deck; the railing was removed and new 4×4 posts were added to support the roof. The decking was replaced with tongue-and-groove flooring to keep the insects out.

AN OUTDOOR KITCHEN

If your climate permits, consider adding an outdoor kitchen. Since these kitchens are exposed to the elements, be sure to use materials made to withstand the weather. Also, make or buy covers for the more vulnerable features, such as the sink or grill. The plumbing and electrical work should be done, or at least approved, by a professional contractor to ensure it's weatherproof. A built-in or portable gas grill with overhead shading makes cooking more comfortable on hot, sunny days. You'll also need to reinforce the deck to support the additional weight of built-in features.

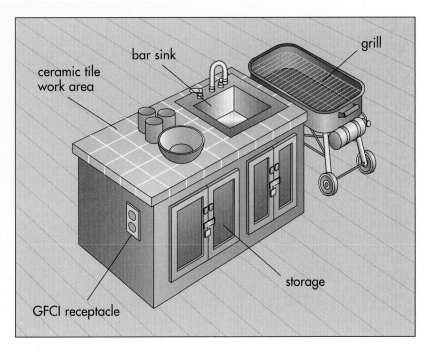

DESIGNING VERSATILITY INTO CONTEMPORARY

*T*humb through a book about traditional houses and you will notice a strong emphasis on the front of the house. Fast forward to any of the dozens of magazines devoted to modern housing and the focus more often than not will be on the back of the house and backyard activities.

Decks are a relatively recent architectural innovation. Many traditional house styles featured a covered porch at the front entry, which welcomed visitors and allowed the residents a platform for observing the passing scene. Today, the traffic outside the front door is less pedestrian and much noisier. We prefer the quiet and privacy of a backyard deck.

Decks can be designed to suit almost any house, but the simplest deck projects match contemporary house styles just as they meet contemporary life styles.

This deck on a contemporary lakeside house combines the shelter of a traditional covered porch with the expansiveness of a deck. With the roof as a linking element and the same stain used throughout, the deck blends right in. Steps unify the porch and the various levels and provide informal seating for gatherings.

EXPERTS' INSIGHT

PLAN FOR PRIVACY

For all its good design, a deck can fall into disuse because of a crucial oversight—a lack of privacy. If attaching a deck to your house restricts you from putting it in a secluded area, here are some ways you can make up for a lack of privacy:

■ Wrap the deck around to a secluded side of the house.

■ Build a deck-mounted privacy fence.

■ Plant fast-growing shrubbery to screen out noise and unpleasant views.

■ Consider a freestanding deck in a remote area of the yard away from the house.

Smartly placed decks make excellent transition spaces. Here a well-placed fenced deck adds a private, shady space between the house and the most public space of a sun-filled patio. Plantings help blend the deck and patio structures and add bursts of color.

This commodious deck wraps around the back and side of a California cottage-style home. Location is everything: This deck overlooks a big, lush yard. Both kitchen and master bedroom open onto this sweeping space that's big enough to accommodate the owner's frequent outdoor dinner parties. This type of house-embracing deck replaces walkways around the house and readily copes with large gatherings, welcoming visitors with open space.

This front-of-the-house deck was built on a lot described as one only a mountain goat could love. The deck not only adds contemporary simplicity to a traditional style home, it provides access to a front veranda, sunny sitting space, and even parking space. Unobtrusive as a grassy front yard, the deck is a significant improvement to the house.

When planning your deck, think of it as an outdoor living room, not simply a blank helipad. Mentally add the items that could make your deck more livable and more enjoyable. Consider all of the options for seating, shading, lighting, eating, cooking, playing, and relaxing. You may not be able to incorporate all the things you'd like, but with planning it's possible to unobtrusively pack in a lot of features.

COMPLEMENTING YOUR HOME'S STYLE

*B*egin planning your design by studying your house and its immediate environment. Check at the library or in bookstores for books on house styles. Research the defining characteristics of your house. For example, a ranch house is low and flat, a split level has a stepped profile, New England styles are boxy, while bungalows are compact yet neatly crafted. Look for a theme in the design of your house that can be carried over into the deck design, whether it be shape, architectural detail, proportion, or color. Try to match or complement the horizontal and vertical lines of the house. If you end up with a finished project that doesn't shout "New deck!" and has all the functionality you hoped for, you've done a good job.

ABOVE: Bigger isn't always better. Case in point: The small backyard of this house would be overwhelmed by an expansive deck. A well-proportioned deck graced with an arbor and a fence provide an elegant, private outdoor room. The grey and white paint scheme neatly complements the home's color.

EXPERTS' INSIGHT

HIRING A DESIGNER

A professional designer can help you decide how your deck should look and how it should be put together. Even if you plan to build the deck yourself, hiring a designer may be wise. A difficult site or complex deck may require (sometimes by your building code) the services of an architect and, perhaps, an engineer. Many large home centers now offer deck design services, which may include computer-generated drawings with a list of materials needed for construction. You may be lucky enough to live near a lumberyard staffed with experienced employees who can help you make design decisions.

BELOW: As knowledgeable designers know, you can only experience something through being exposed to its opposite. The bank of doors on this ranch house are a beautiful feature. Why fight them? A simple platform-like deck complements the doors and lends the illusion of spaciousness to a small house. As you think about your design, consider contrasts like this as well as the similarities.

ABOVE: *The use and abuse decks receive can make a paint job show its age quickly. Color can be added through the choice of stains. Or you may want to add paint selectively to some vertical surfaces of the deck, such as rail posts or balusters, where it won't have to contend with foot traffic. The dark green decking melds with the house and gives the deck a traditional look. Color also can be added by carefully choosing the deck accessories, such as chairs, tables, and awnings.*

RIGHT: *A hefty and nicely detailed railing gives this low-slung deck substance. It also adds a touch of traditional appeal to the somewhat bland exterior of this ranch-style home. Sometimes such detailing can direct the eye away from undesirable features. In the design phase, don't be afraid to experiment with various options like this.*

DESIGNING DECKS FOR ANY SITUATION

Many homeowners do not live on lots ideally suited for decks. If your property appears too narrow, shallow, or sloped, or if you have a less-than-desirable view nearby, don't despair. Working within some constraints can bring out creative solutions.

Problem sites often require the services of a professional designer and a licensed builder as well. Often, a deck can cover an unusable outdoor space, such as a steep terraced slope, transforming it into a comfortable and functional addition to your house.

Sometimes the problems are not due to the site but are created by the layout of the house or its proximity to neighbors. Wraparound decks can link areas of the house. Decks also can be designed to face away from and screen unsightly areas.

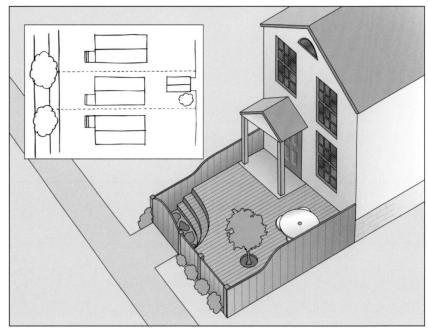

Use all of a narrow lot.
Decks on narrow lots with close neighbors often are built no larger than the width of the house. Here, a deck completely fills a narrow city lot, putting a limited front yard to good use. High screens wrapping the structure keep the deck area private and buffer unwanted street noise.

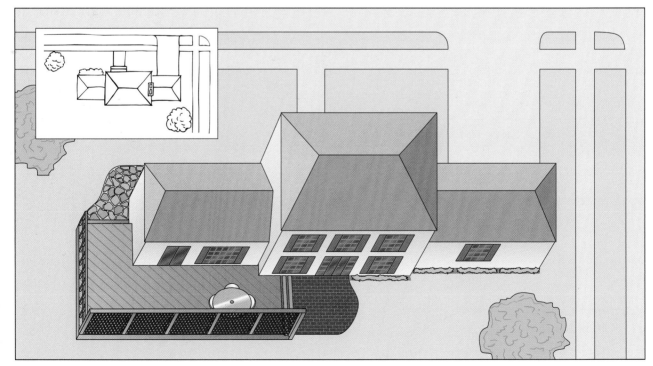

Build long and narrow on a shallow lot.
A lot that doesn't lend itself to an expansive deck doesn't mean you can't have a deck. Think creatively. A long, narrow deck might just fit the bill. This deck wraps around the side of the house and includes a stone walk to the front. The design centers on a sliding door for access to the house and includes screening to maintain privacy. A small patio extends the usable space and adds another level of use and interest.

Block an unsightly view.

All too often people store things along the edges of their property, often right up against a neighbor's lot. Unsightly piles of stuff may be out of sight for them but right up against the space you want to use for outdoor living. By anticipating views and adjusting your design in advance, you can screen out unpleasant vistas. This deck not only includes an attached privacy fence, but the deck is angled so activity, seating, and the natural flow of traffic cause people to look away from the lot next door. Everything is directed toward the most desirable area of the lot.

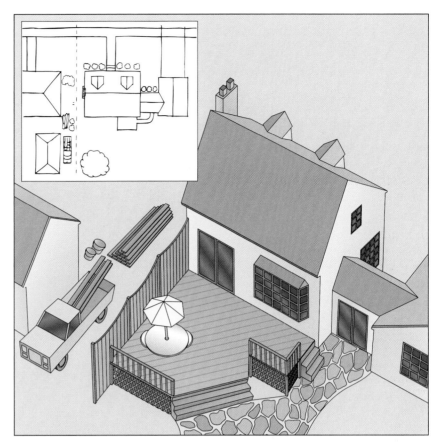

Take advantage of a steep slope.

Steep slopes are both an advantage and a disadvantage. Because the ground drops quickly away from the house, a deck on a steep slope can offer wonderful views. But, such decks can be difficult to build. Whether the ground slopes down or up from the site, a multilevel deck that follows the ground's contour is usually the best solution. It gives complexity to the feel of the deck and reduces the height of the outer edge of the deck, therefore decreasing the difficulty of construction.

CAUTION!
CONSULT AN ENGINEER
Elevated decks on steep slopes require sophisticated foundations and framing. Designing such a deck may require assessments of soil integrity, drainage, and earthquake vulnerability. In this case, call in a professional.

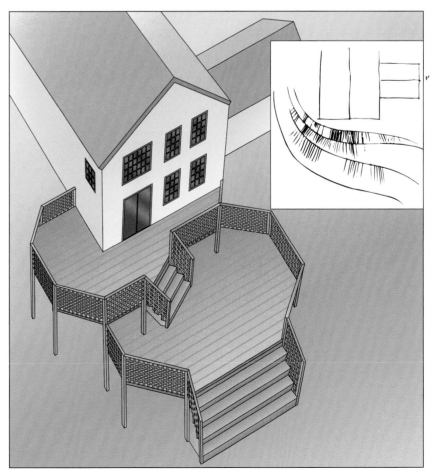

PREPARING FOR THE PROJECT

The transition from theory to practice can be the most difficult phase of a deck-building project. This is the point where doubts may start to plague you.

■ Will the deck be big enough?
■ Can I really afford to build it?
■ Do I have the skills needed to build a deck?

Listen carefully to the doubts and try to answer them thoroughly before proceeding. Don't rush into the project. Think through all of the procedures and consequences. If you've recently moved into the house, it might be too soon to build a deck. By waiting a full year, you'll have time to observe the house and yard through a full course of seasonal changes and weather conditions.

Budgeting is a tricky—and highly personal—part of the project. With thorough planning, however, you can avoid surprises. As long as you supply all of the labor, you can determine your out-of-pocket expenses by preparing a detailed list of materials (drawn from your equally detailed plans), which you can take to several suppliers for estimates. If your budget is tight, only you can decide if you want to borrow the money and build today or save your money and build tomorrow.

Deck building is straightforward work. But parts of it are physically demanding, and all of it requires close attention to detail. If you remain concerned about your ability to build the deck you want, narrow down those parts of the job that trouble you the most.

Perhaps you worry about getting the ledger installed correctly or the posts set plumb and in a straight line. If so, take on the role of general contractor and subcontract parts of the job. You may be able to hire an experienced carpenter to do those segments of the job that you feel uncomfortable about. This mini-apprenticeship may be all you need to boost your confidence for tackling your next remodeling project.

No matter how long it takes, resolve your doubts before ordering lumber. Once that delivery truck backs into your driveway, you want to have a building permit in hand, a clear idea of what your deck will look like, and a plan for who's going to handle the work.

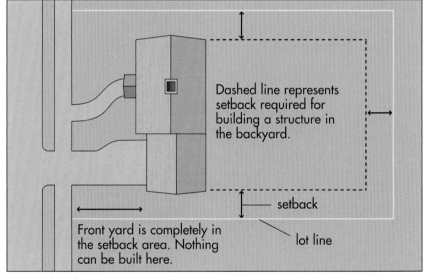

Dashed line represents setback required for building a structure in the backyard.

setback

lot line

Front yard is completely in the setback area. Nothing can be built here.

Keep it legal.
Like most major home improvements, a deck addition must be done in compliance with local building codes and zoning laws. Submit plans to your town or county building department for approval and to obtain a building permit. Depending on its policies, the building department also may require inspections to make sure you're following the approved plans. This legal supervision ensures that your design will be built properly. Remember, building codes prevent your neighbors from doing things you might not like. Failing to comply with codes could result in having to remove what you've built.

Not everyone is covered by zoning laws or required to get a building permit. But it's up to you, not the authorities, to find out what laws cover your project.

Play it safe.

The elements that make decks useful, fun, and good-looking, such as stairways, railings, multiple levels, hot tubs, or high elevations, also create safety hazards, especially for children. Complying with local building codes doesn't guarantee a safe deck. Legal requirements represent minimal standards; your situation may demand more. Minimize risks by observing these precautions:

■ When building a deck railing, space the balusters no more than 4 inches apart, even if your local code allows wider spacing.

■ Treat deck stairs the same as indoor stairs; if young children are around, put a gate at the top and bottom.

■ If you install built-in benches, make the railings behind them at least 24 inches above the seat to prevent a child from climbing or tipping over the side.

■ Hot tubs should be fenced off with a childproof gate. If that's not practical, use a secured cover.

Space balusters no more than 4 inches apart

Add gate to stairs.

Place outdoor furniture as you plan to use it on the deck.

Mark levels.

Flour marks outline of deck.

Make a trial run.

Mark the perimeter of your deck and its various levels with flour. Place your lawn furniture inside the perimeter to get a feel for how much space you need. Use strings to indicate railing heights. Set the string lines at the height of the proposed deck to give you a sense of its profile.

Money $ Saver

TAKE A SHORTCUT

■ You may be surprised at the time- and money-saving services available at your local home center or lumberyard. They may offer ready-made plans, either sold individually or collected in book form. If you find a plan you like and your building site presents no unusual problems, the cost of printed plans can be money well spent.

■ If you want a simple deck that's neither large nor fitted with many custom features, consider buying a precut deck kit. Some larger home centers and lumberyards offer these complete deck packages at attractive prices.

ORGANIZING ESSENTIAL TOOLS

One of the nice things about building a deck is that you don't have to spend a lot of money buying specialized tools. In fact, you already may have all of the tools you'll need for the job.

Few tools will see more action than a flexible 25- or 30-foot **tape measure.** A 1-inch-wide tape extends farther and lasts longer than a ½-inch tape. Some carpenters prefer a folding ruler for smaller jobs. Look for one with a metal extension used for inside measurements. Use a chisel-pointed **carpenter's pencil** to make your marks and avoid endless pencil sharpening.

A **framing square** (also called a carpenter's square) is used to check corners for square and to mark stair stringers and roof rafters. A smaller **speed square** allows you to quickly figure angled

cuts. It's a tough and compact tool that holds its shape even when banged around. It slips into your back pocket and is handy for quickly marking cut lines on lumber. Some carpenters use the square as a cutting guide with a circular saw. A **combination square** is helpful for scribing lines. A **T-bevel** can be set to duplicate any angle.

A **carpenter's level** is an indispensable tool for checking level and plumb. A 4-foot level is the best choice for deck building, although you can get by with a 2-foot one. Use **mason's line** and a **line level** to lay out level footings or other excavations. A **plumb bob** establishes vertical lines. Snap long, straight lines in an instant with a **chalk line,** which can double as a plumb bob.

Buy a **hammer** that is

comfortable and solidly built. The most popular models weigh 16 ounces and have curved claws. You may find a baffling array of specialty hammers, but stick with a basic one. The curved claw enables you to remove nails easily. If you have a lot of nails to pull (when recycling some boards or dismantling part of an old deck for repair), you may want to use a **cat's paw.** A flat **pry bar** also removes nails and comes in handy for levering warped deck boards into line. Use a **nail set** to sink the heads of finishing nails.

A **wood chisel** enables you to clean out notches in posts. A **utility knife** with a retractable blade is standard carpenter's equipment. A **plane** is useful for shaving wood off the edge of a board or smoothing sharp edges on a post or railing.

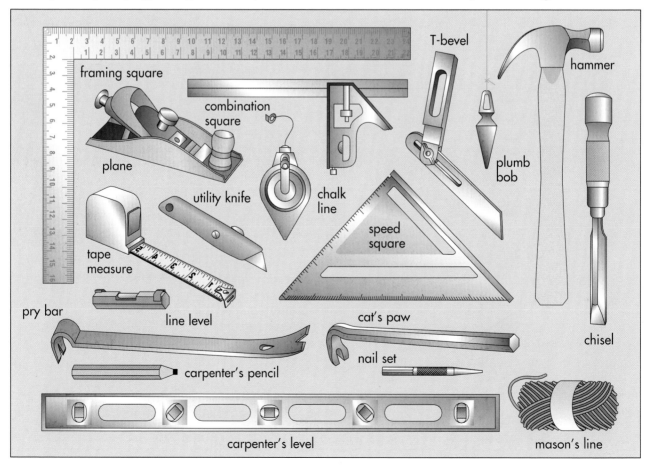

framing square · combination square · plane · utility knife · chalk line · T-bevel · hammer · plumb bob · speed square · tape measure · chisel · pry bar · line level · cat's paw · nail set · carpenter's pencil · carpenter's level · mason's line

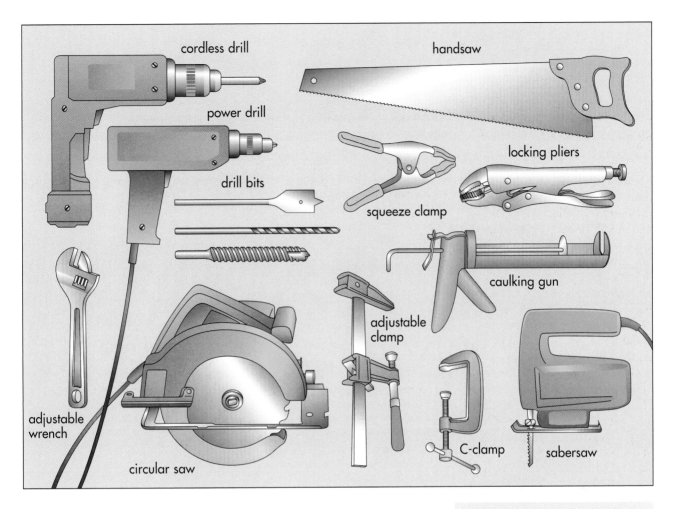

cordless drill

handsaw

power drill

locking pliers

drill bits

squeeze clamp

caulking gun

adjustable clamp

adjustable wrench

C-clamp

sabersaw

circular saw

Be sure to buy a **power drill** that has variable speed and is reversible. For most do-it-yourselfers, a ⅜-inch chuck suffices. Keyless chucks make changing bits quick and easy, but some people prefer the tighter grip they can get using a keyed chuck. **Cordless drills** keep improving, and carpenters are relying on them more and more. You will need a set of **drill bits** to drill holes and screwdriver bits for driving screws.

Although you probably will do most of your cutting with power tools, a **handsaw** still comes in handy. You may want to choose a smaller saw that fits into a toolbox. To fasten nuts, bolts, and lag screws, use an **adjustable wrench.** A pair of **locking pliers** helps to hold fasteners or pieces of wood tight while you work.

A good supply of clamps always comes in handy on a construction job. **C-clamps** come in a variety of sizes and can handle most any job. **Squeeze clamps** are inexpensive, quick to use, and less likely to dent lumber. A quick-fitting **adjustable clamp** is handy for holding thick pieces of lumber.

A **circular saw** crosscuts, angle cuts, rips (cuts lengthwise), and even bevels lumber easily and cleanly. Look for a saw rated at 12 or 13 amps that uses 7¼-inch blades. An all-purpose blade is fine for deck building.

If you need to cut into the siding on your house to attach the ledger, you will want to seal the opening with flashing and some caulk. For the latter, you'll need an inexpensive **caulking gun.**

If you decide to shop for a **sabersaw,** examine the base plate and the mechanism for adjusting it. On cheaper saws, these are flimsy and will wobble eventually, making it difficult to keep the blade aligned vertically.

USING A CIRCULAR SAW

The circular saw is the single most indispensable tool for building a deck. As quality has improved and prices have fallen, the circular saw has become a staple for most do-it-yourselfers. It requires minimal maintenance, has a short learning curve, and is relatively safe to use. This versatile tool is capable of ripping, crosscutting, straightening edges, plowing out notches, and cutting bevels. You'll need this tool not only for such straightforward tasks as trimming deck boards but for making plunge cuts into siding to make room for ledger boards (see page 37) and for trimming posts (see page 45).

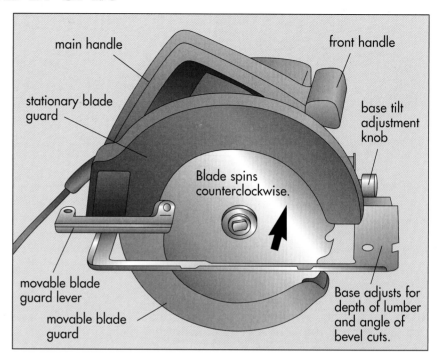

main handle · front handle · stationary blade guard · base tilt adjustment knob · Blade spins counterclockwise. · movable blade guard lever · movable blade guard · Base adjusts for depth of lumber and angle of bevel cuts.

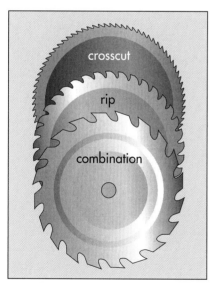

crosscut · rip · combination

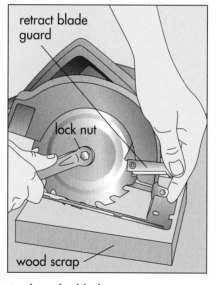

retract blade guard · lock nut · wood scrap

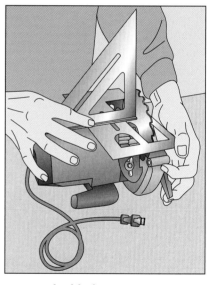

Choose the correct blade.

A fine-tooth crosscut blade is suited for cutting across the grain. It also makes smooth, clean cuts in plywood. A rip blade is best for cutting with the grain, such as lengthwise on wide 2× lumber. A combination blade is standard-issue on new saws. It can be used to both rip and crosscut and is the best choice if you don't want to change blades regularly.

Replace the blade.

Note: *Unplug the saw.* When removing a blade, set the saw on a piece of scrap and push down so the blade will not turn. With a wrench (usually supplied with a new saw), loosen the locking nut. Carefully remove the nut and blade. Insert the new blade with the teeth at the front of the saw pointing upward, and tighten the nut. If the blade is secured with washers, be sure to replace them in the proper order.

Square the blade.

Note: *Unplug the saw.* Circular saws can be adjusted to cut up to a 45-degree angle, but most of your cutting will be square. Ignore the degree settings stamped on the angle adjustment mechanism; they are seldom accurate. Instead, drop the blade as far below the base plate as possible, then adjust the baseplate using a speed square. When the blade is perfectly aligned with the vertical edge of the square, tighten the baseplate.

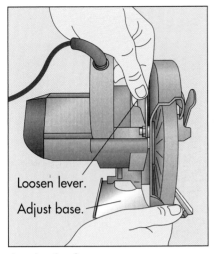

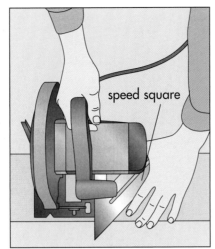

Set depth of cut.

Note: *Unplug the saw.* Tool manufacturers often suggest the saw blade be set to project no more than ¼ inch beneath the surface being cut. Carpenters often prefer to have a full saw tooth extending beneath the surface. The latter approach exposes more of the spinning blade, but it allows for quicker sawdust removal from within the cut. Once you set the depth, tighten the locking lever.

Make straight cuts.

Many carpenters learn to make straight cuts by keeping a close eye on the pencil line. Others find they achieve greater accuracy by using a speed square placed against the baseplate to guide the saw. There's no perfect technique; practice until you find a method with which you can produce consistently square cuts.

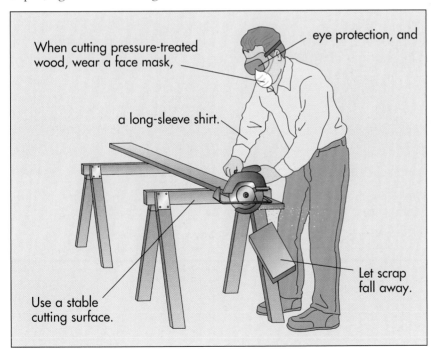

When cutting pressure-treated wood, wear a face mask,

a long-sleeve shirt.

eye protection, and

Let scrap fall away.

Use a stable cutting surface.

Support your work.

Traditionally, the first thing a carpenter's apprentice learned to build was a pair of sawhorses. Whether you make or buy your own, use them. Cut long boards so

that the cutoff falls off the end. Never make cuts between the sawhorses, which can cause the saw to bind and kick back dangerously. Use clamps or a free hand to support the work.

SAFE WORKING HABITS

In addition to wearing protective gear, you can minimize the potential hazards of deck building in the following ways:

■ Set up a spacious work area. Keep it free of loose lumber and construction waste

■ Stop working when you feel tired; take a break or quit for the day.

■ Never work when under the influence of alcohol or drugs, including cold medicines.

■ Lift properly, bending at the knees and using your legs rather than your back.

■ Select the proper tool for the job, read the operator's manual, and use the tool correctly.

■ Maintain all your tools; keep cutting tools sharp and store them safely.

■ Climb no higher than the third step from the top of a step or extension ladder.

■ Don't lean out from a ladder.

■ Store flammable liquids in approved containers. Never store them in glass bottles.

■ Make sure all power tools are either double-insulated or grounded. Double-insulated tools provide the best protection. They usually are marked as such and have a two-pronged plug because they don't need grounding.

■ To guard against shock, make sure all power tools are connected to a ground-fault circuit interrupter (GFCI). GFCIs may be built into an existing outlet, or you can use a portable model.

■ Use only extension cords rated to handle the amperage load, and use the shortest cord possible for the job at hand.

■ Keep oily rags and similar wastes in a tightly sealed metal container; rags left in a pile may combust spontaneously.

USING A POWER DRILL

When building a deck, you must drill many holes for bolts and pilot holes for screws. A power drill and a supply of sharp twist and spade bits make this chore a lot easier. With a supply of screwdriver bits you can turn your variable-speed power drill or cordless drill into a power screwdriver. Professionals often keep several drills at hand on the job site. Even an amateur deck builder can find uses for more than one drill; for example, a corded drill for heavy duty work and a cordless drill for lighter chores.

Don't overheat the bit. If you see smoke, stop drilling. Pause once in a while and check for overheating. If the bit or the drill itself is too hot, you probably are pushing too hard. With deep holes, lift the bit out of the hole every so often to clear sawdust out of the hole. Hold the drill upright as you work. Tipping the tool while drilling may break the bit.

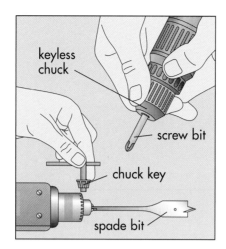

Choose your chuck.
If you buy a new drill, it probably will have a keyless chuck. Keyless chucks allow you to change bits by simply turning the chuck with your hand. While they spare you the trouble of fumbling around with the key, they often don't hold the bit as tightly as needed. Keyed chucks are still available and offer the tightest grip. You can buy an adapter that turns your keyed chuck into a keyless chuck.

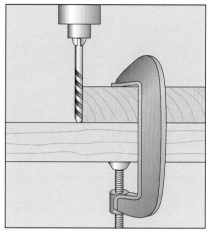

Add a guide for straight holes.
Usually, you'll want to drill holes perpendicular to the board. Check the bit for square as it enters the material by clamping a piece of square-cut scrap lumber in place, as shown. With some drills you can hold a square on the material and against the body of the drill. The ability to drill straight holes is vital to good carpentry, so practice your technique.

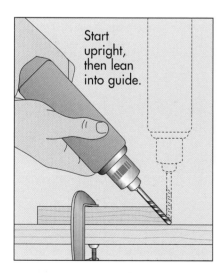

Improvise a guide for angled holes.
Make a guide for angled holes by cutting the edge of a piece of scrap lumber to the desired angle. Clamp the guide so it aligns with the tip of the bit exactly on your hole mark. Begin the hole by drilling perpendicular, then shift the drill to the correct angle.

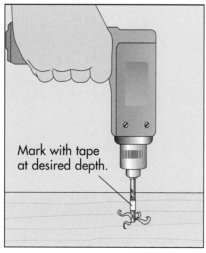

Mark the bit for depth.
When you want to drill one or more holes to a certain depth, wrap tape around the drill bit so the bottom edge of the tape contacts the material at the desired depth. Drill with gentle pressure. Back the bit out when the tape touches the surface of the material.

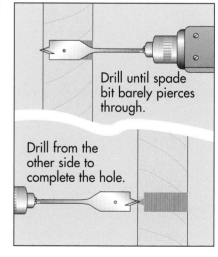

Double drill bolt holes.
A spade bit tends to tear the wood as it drills through the other side. For clean bores, use this two-step technique. Choose a bit slightly larger than the bolt diameter. Drill through one side until the tip breaks through. Then move to the other side and finish drilling.

MEASURING AND LEVELING

There's a good reason why the first rule of carpentry is, "Measure twice, cut once." Small mistakes add up, producing sloppy results. If you don't catch the error, you may throw the whole deck out of whack and have to dismantle it and rebuild.

All carpentry projects require that you understand how to establish level references. The art of finding level isn't just for the purpose of creating flat surfaces, it is also necessary for ensuring accurate measurements. A tape measure works only along two dimensions. If you aren't measuring along a level surface, the measurement is compromised. For example, if you lay out your deck by measuring from the house along a sloping yard, rather than along a level plane, you could wind up with dimensions several inches, or even several feet, wrong.

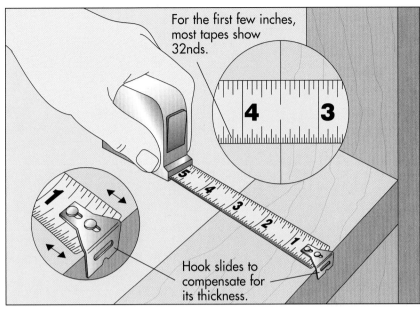

Use a tape measure.
The hook at the end of a tape measure slides back and forth slightly to compensate for its own thickness. This means that whether you hook the tape on a board end for an outside measurement or push it against a flat surface for an inside measurement, the reading is still accurate. The first few inches of many tape measures are divided into $\frac{1}{32}$-inch increments for detailed measurements.

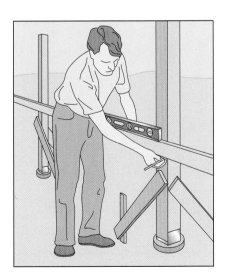

Extend the level with a board.
To establish level between posts, place a carpenter's level on the edge of a straight board. Site down the board to make sure it is straight. If necessary, use tape to keep the level centered on the board. With a carpenter's level, you know you have a level surface when the bubble in the horizontal vial centers between the two lines.

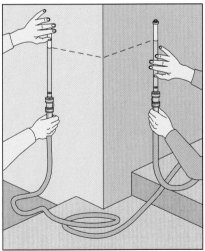

Use a water level for large spans.
Used properly, a water level is an unerringly accurate tool for finding level. Although not necessary on smaller decks, it may be indispensable for large decks or for checking level around corners. You can make a water level with plastic tubing filled with water, or you can buy a commercial model like the one shown.

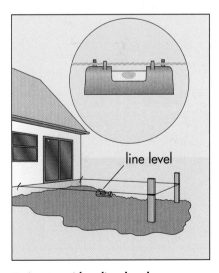

Estimate with a line level.
Inexpensive line levels are handy for making rough estimates, but they are not as accurate as a carpenter's level or a water level. Clip the level on a mason's line, then adjust the line until the level's bubble is centered. The line must be as taut as possible, and there should be little if any wind affecting the mason's line.

USING SPECIALIZED TOOLS

Sometimes one of the toughest and potentially most expensive decisions you have to make on a building project is which, if any, new tools to buy. It seldom makes sense to buy high-priced power tools if you don't expect to use them regularly in the years to come. On the other hand, having access to good power tools makes the project go faster and often results in a better job.

One rule of thumb is to buy only one new power tool at a time. Learn how to use it safely and master its range of functions before making another investment. Many do-it-yourselfers like to look at each new project as an opportunity to add a new tool to their collection. Remember, needing a tool doesn't always mean having to buy it; you may be able to borrow the tool from a friend or neighbor. When that's not possible, consider renting.

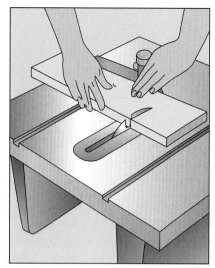

Use a tablesaw for many cuts.
For long, straight cuts, it's hard to beat a tablesaw. Use it for dado cuts as well. It also works for crosscutting narrow boards and miter cutting, although not as efficiently as a power miter saw. A tablesaw can be especially useful for mass producing balusters or stair treads.

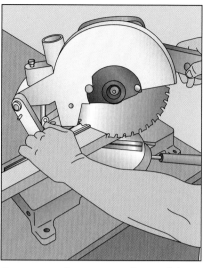

A power miter saw makes quick, precise cuts.
This tool, also called a chopsaw or cutoff saw, makes quick, precise crosscuts and miter cuts. It excels at repetitive tasks, such as cutting dozens of equally long balusters. A model with a 10-inch blade will suffice for deck-building projects.

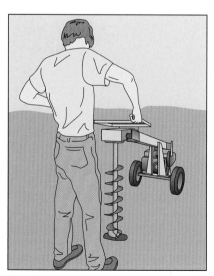

To dig postholes, rent a one-person power auger, ...
To dig holes quickly, rent a power auger. If you must dig holes by yourself and want to avoid the work required of a clamshell posthole digger (see page 42), use this one-person unit. You'll need a trailer hitch to haul it home.

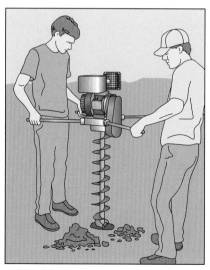

a hand-held power auger, ...
Two-person motorized augers take a lot of muscle power to control. Be sure to get thorough instructions when you rent the machine. Be braced for hitting roots and rocks. As you work, you'll need to lift out the unit to occasionally clear the auger.

or a trailer-mounted power auger.
This hydraulic-powered unit offers maximum boring power with minimum wear and tear on the operator. To ease the auger into the earth, you simply turn a steering-wheel-like mechanism. The unit bears the brunt of the strain of lifting and lowering.

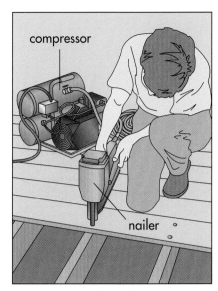

Rent a pneumatic nailer.
Essentially a power hammer, a pneumatic nailer is a standard tool for professional carpenters. It's not a tool most do-it-yourselfers could justify buying; but if you must nail on lots of decking, this is a tool well worth renting. Some practice is necessary to get nails to set at the right depth.

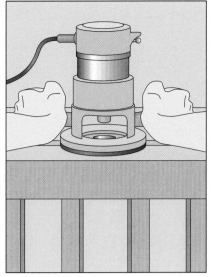

Use a router for rounding edges.
If you ask most experienced woodworkers to name their favorite tool, a large percentage of them will say it's their router. A router is useful when building a deck for cutting dadoes and rounding over the sharp edges on posts, handrails, and stair treads.

RENTING TOOLS

When you need an expensive tool for only a short period or if you can't afford to buy it new, a tool rental store can save the day. A reasonably well-equipped rental shop carries virtually any power tool you'll find in this book, including circular saws and drills. When contemplating tool purchases, it pays to compare the costs of buying new versus renting.

If you have doubts about how to use a tool, the advice you receive from rental store personnel often is far more comprehensive than what you'll find in an owner's manual. Tools are rented by the hour, day, or week. To avoid excessive charges, don't pick up the tool until you need it. Clean the tool before returning it to avoid extra charges.

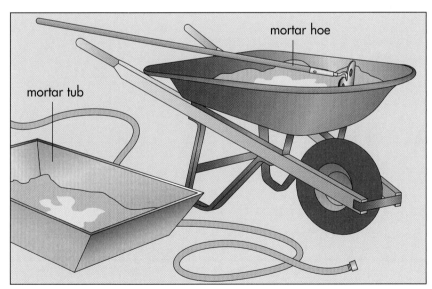

Mix concrete in a mortar tub.
Mixing concrete is a process of blending dry ingredients with water. For large projects, you can save money by mixing the dry ingredients (Portland cement, sand, and stone or gravel) yourself. However, premixed 60-pound bags are the best choice for most deck projects. In either case, you'll need a large tub in which to mix the concrete. A wheelbarrow is mobile, but a mortar tub is cheaper and holds more concrete. A mortar hoe has holes in its face, allowing for more efficient mixing, but you can get by with a standard garden hoe or shovel. You'll also need a source of water and a mason's trowel.

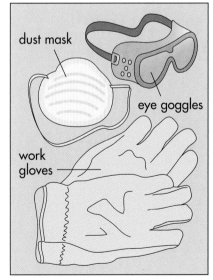

Use safety wear.
Wear work gloves when handling lumber, especially pressure-treated lumber. But take them off when operating a power tool. Eye goggles always should be worn when using power tools and are recommended when hammering. When sanding or grinding, protect your lungs with a dust mask.

CHOOSING AND BUYING LUMBER

As you learn carpentry skills, it's important to become familiar with the characteristics and uses of types of lumber, and choosing the wood that will work best for a certain project. Here's what you need to know to get the best material.

For construction purposes, there are two general classes of wood: Softwood, which comes from evergreen trees, and hardwood, which comes from deciduous trees. Wood that has been cut and milled to size generally is referred to as lumber. The most commonly used lumber on decks comes from softwood trees, such as pine, fir, cedar, and redwood. Lumber is graded according to how many knots it has and the quality of its surface (see chart *below*).

No matter what species of lumber you buy, watch for the wood flaws pictured at *right*. A board that is heavily twisted, bowed, cupped, or crooked is seldom usable, although some bows flatten out as you nail the boards in place. Knots are only a cosmetic problem, unless they are loose and likely to pop out. Checking, which is a rift in the surface, also is only cosmetic. Splits cannot be repaired and will widen in time. Cut them off.

Lumber is ordered in nominal sizes, but the actual dimension will be less (see chart, *page 29*). Large quantities of lumber are sometimes figured by the board foot. A board foot is the wood equivalent of a piece 12 nominal inches square and 1 inch thick (see chart *below*).

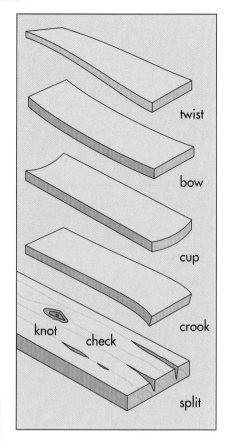

twist

bow

cup

crook

knot   check

split

SOME COMMON GRADES OF WOOD

Clear	Has no knots
Select or select structural	High-quality wood; broken down into No. 1, No. 2, and No. 3, or A, B, C, and D; lower grades have more knots.
No. 2 common	Has tight knots, no major blemishes; good for shelving.
No. 3 common	Some knots may be loose; often blemished or damaged.
Construction or standard	Good strength; used for general framing.
Utility	Economy grade used for rough framing.

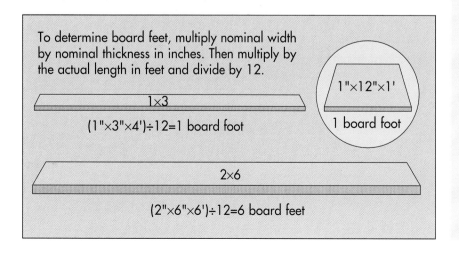

To determine board feet, multiply nominal width by nominal thickness in inches. Then multiply by the actual length in feet and divide by 12.

1×3

(1"×3"×4')÷12=1 board foot

1"×12"×1'

1 board foot

2×6

(2"×6"×6')÷12=6 board feet

EXPERTS' INSIGHT

INSPECT BEFORE BUYING
If you order lumber by telephone, you will get someone else's choice of boards, not your own. Lumberyards usually have plenty of substandard wood lying around. The only way to be sure you do not get some of it is to pick out the boards yourself. Some lumberyards will not allow you to sort through the stack because they want to keep the wood stacked neatly—the only way to keep lumber from warping. But they should at least let you stand by and approve the selection. Failing that, confirm that you can return boards you don't like.

COMMON DECK LUMBER CHOICES

LUMBER TYPE	CHARACTERISTICS
Pressure-treated pine (sometimes fir)	Readily available in large variety of sizes; resistant to rot and pests; strong, fairly easy to work with; available with waterproofing finish already applied; accepts all exterior stains.
Western red cedar	Heartwood naturally resistant to rot and pests; appealing golden brown appearance, but weathers to grayish tones unless treated with clear wood finish; structurally weak, best avoided for posts, beams, and joists; not available everywhere; costs considerably more than pressure-treated lumber.
Redwood	Heartwood naturally resistant to rot and pests, including termites; deep red color that weathers to silvery gray if left unfinished; relatively soft, but can be used for all parts of a deck; expensive outside of the West Coast.
Plastic wood	New product, frequently manufactured as a composite of wood and plastic; most commonly used as decking, not for structural members; cuts and fastens much like standard lumber; long-lasting and won't splinter; as a new material it's best to investigate performance of products sold in your area.

HANDLING TREATED WOOD

Pressure-treated lumber has been saturated with chemical preservatives, which are deeply embedded in the wood's fibers under pressure. The wood-treating industry claims that, when properly treated and allowed to dry, pressure-treated wood is safe to handle and the chemicals will not leach out of the wood. Nevertheless, when working with pressure-treated lumber, observe the following precautions:

▪ Wear gloves when handling it, except if you are operating a power tool.
▪ Wear a dust mask and goggles when cutting it.
▪ Wash your hands before eating, drinking, or smoking.
▪ Never burn the wood, especially in a wood stove.
▪ Dispose of wood scraps with regular trash.
▪ Don't use such wood indoors.
▪ Launder work clothes separately from other clothing, especially baby clothing and diapers.

MEASUREMENTS

UNDERSTANDING DIMENSIONAL LUMBER

Lumber is referred to by its rough size before being milled to finished dimensions. Use this "nominal" sizes when ordering, but keep "actual" sizes in mind when measuring.

Nominal Size	Actual Size
2×2	1½×1½
2×4	1½×3½
2×6	1½×5½
2×8	1½×7½
4×4	3½×3½
6×6	5½×5½

MIX AND MATCH

Different parts of a deck have different functions and levels of visibility, so it isn't necessary to build an entire deck out of a single type of wood. Unless you live on the West Coast, where prices for redwood may allow for its use for structural members, the best choice for posts, beams, and joists usually is pressure-treated lumber. A decay-resistant species can then be used for the decking and railing. If you want to maximize the visual appeal of your deck, keep in mind that the railing most likely will be the most evident component from street level.

CALCULATING SPANS

Posts, beams, joists, and decking comprise the structural members of a deck. Their spacing and sizing are critical to ensuring a deck is safe and secure. Building codes vary, and it is up to you to contact your local building department for guidance in designing your deck.

When calculating allowable spans be aware that specifications vary depending on the type of wood you use. Also, spans often change for a deck that is higher than 12 feet. And when you change the size or spacing of one structural member, it can affect the size and spacing of others. For example, you could use fewer posts, spaced farther apart, if you use a larger beam.

The table at *right* lists spans typically allowed for pressure-treated (pt) Southern yellow pine. The calculations that produce these spans assume that the deck must support a load of 50 pounds per square foot. That figure breaks down into 10 pounds per square foot of "dead weight" (the weight of the construction materials) and 40 pounds per square foot of "live weight" (the weight of people and objects on the deck).

WOOD STRENGTH VARIES

Species and grades of wood vary in strength. Design your framing with the strength of the wood in mind. Southern yellow pine and Douglas fir have the same allowable spans and are the most common types of pressure-treated lumber. Redwood and Western red cedar are weaker and also need shorter spans. Check with your local lumberyard or home center for the types of lumber available and suitable for use in your area.

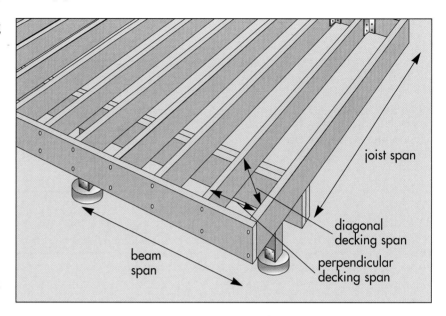

joist span

diagonal decking span

perpendicular decking span

beam span

DECK LUMBER SPANS

BEAM SPANS FOR PT SOUTHERN YELLOW PINE
Maximum Beam Span Between Posts Based on On-Center Distance Between Beams or Ledger to Beam

Nominal Beam Size	4'	5'	6'	7'	8'	9'	10'	11'	12'
(2) 2×6	7'	6'							
4×6	7'	7'	6'						
(2) 2×8	9'	8'	7'	7'	6'	6'			
4×8	10'	9'	8'	7'	7'	6'	6'	6'	
(2) 2×10	11'	10'	9'	8'	8'	7'	7'	6'	6'
(2) 2×12	13'	12'	10'	10'	9'	8'	8'	7'	7'

JOIST SPANS FOR PT SOUTHERN YELLOW PINE
Maximum Joist Spans Based on Joist Spacing

Nominal Joist Size	12" Joist Spacing	16" Joist Spacing	24" Joist Spacing
2×6	10'4"	9'5"	7'10"
2×8	13'8"	12'5"	10'2"
2×10	17'5"	15'5"	12'7"

DECKING SPANS

Species	Nominal Decking Size	Recommended Span
Redwood, Western red cedar, pressure-treated Southern yellow pine or Douglas fir	⁵⁄₄×4, ⁵⁄₄×6 (radius edge, except Southern yellow pine)	16"
	⁵⁄₄×4, ⁵⁄₄×6 (radius edge, Southern yellow pine)	24"
	2×4, 2×6	24"

CHOOSING HARDWARE

Using the right fasteners is important. This is no place to save a few dollars. Fasteners and connectors must withstand years of exposure without rusting or otherwise weakening their grip. Every fastener should be suitable for long-term exterior use.

Galvanizing is the most common treatment for metal fasteners used outdoors. But there are differences in the methods and materials used in galvanizing. The best process is hot-dip galvanizing, in which the fastener is dipped in molten zinc. The thickest coating of zinc is found on fasteners that meet that standard—ASTM A153.

Stainless steel fasteners cost considerably more, but they are extremely resistant to degradation. Use them near saltwater or other regularly wet or corrosive conditions. Aluminum fasteners are not recommended.

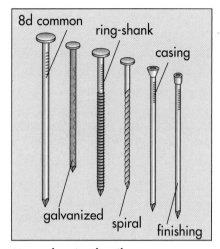

Use galvanized nails.
When nailing on the decking boards, ring- or spiral-shank nails provide a much better grip than common wood nails. On the other hand, they can be difficult to remove if you need to replace decking. Hot-dipped galvanized nails are best for most decks. Use stainless steel for extremely wet or corrosive applications.

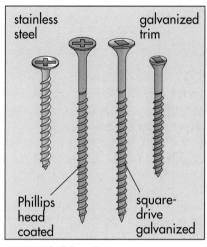

Screws hold well.
Stainless steel, anodized, or hot-dipped galvanized screws are excellent choices for fastening decking. Screws for this purpose often are referred to as decking screws. They are available in 2- to 3-inch lengths, with either Phillips or square-drive heads. Do not use regular black-coated screws intended for wallboard or other interior purposes.

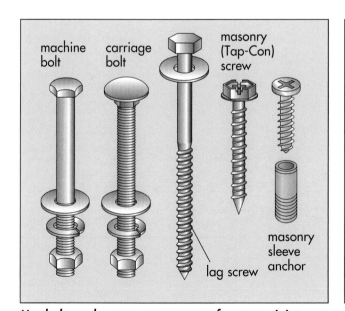

Use bolts and masonry connectors for strong joints.
The strongest fasteners for joining structural members are machine and carriage bolts. Machine bolts require a washer on both ends; carriage bolts require a washer only on the nut end. Carriage bolts have a rounded head. Use ½-inch bolts unless directed otherwise. Lag screws are necessary when access is restricted. Use anchors when fastening ledger boards to masonry or concrete foundations.

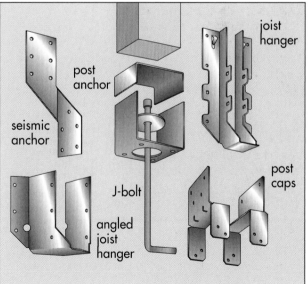

Post and joist connectors simplify joint work.
Ready-made lumber connectors have simplified many aspects of deck construction. Seismic (or hurricane) anchors help secure joists to beams. Post anchors tie posts to the concrete piers via a J-bolt, eliminating the need to embed posts in concrete. Joist hangers offer a secure pocket for joists, while post caps allow a quick means of supporting beams on posts.

PLANNING FOUNDATIONS

The foundation is designed to support the entire load of the deck. All of the construction above the foundation is intended to direct that load into the ground. In most cases, decks are supported by concrete piers set far enough in the ground to remain stable through every season. In some cases, however, posts can be sunk into a small concrete pad at the bottom of the posthole.

Check your local building codes to see what is required. Code requirements are based on local climate and soil conditions and should ensure that your deck will not move with time, twisting away from the house and ruining the integrity of the framing.

Although it requires digging more footings, a freestanding deck (see page 33) is supported next to the house rather than by a ledger on the house. It offers the greatest strength, security, and protection from moisture incursion.

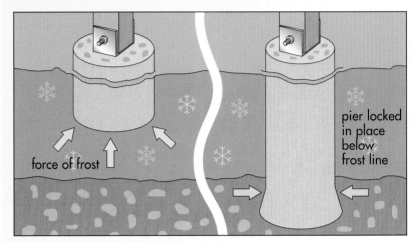

Prevent frost heave.
The foundation must be strong and stable. In cold climates, the effects of frost penetration must be considered in the design of the foundation. If frost is allowed to form beneath a concrete footing or pier, it can push the entire deck up with so much force that it weakens the entire structure. To guard against frost heave, building codes require that the bottom of the foundation rest below the frostline, which is the maximum depth the frost will penetrate. In some parts of the country, this requires foundations to be dug 4 to 5 feet deep. Your local building department can tell you what size and depth your foundation must be.

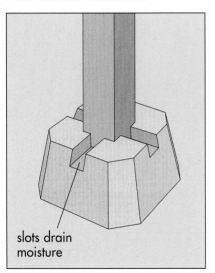

Use precast concrete footings in frost-free areas.
In areas where frost heave isn't a problem, precast concrete footings are the simplest foundation. The footing should sit on compacted or undisturbed soil.

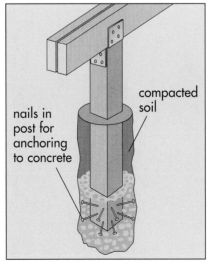

Place post in concrete footing.
This foundation uses only a small amount of concrete to form a footing entirely below the frostline. The post material must be rated for ground contact. Nails in each side hold the post in the concrete. Backfill the remainder of the hole with compacted layers of soil.

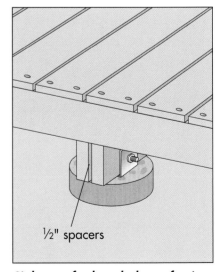

Sit beams for low decks on footing.
Posts are necessary only to raise the deck to the desired height. For low decks, posts can be eliminated. Just set the beams directly in the post anchor. A beam of 2× lumber must be widened with ½-inch spacers to fill a 4×4 post anchor.

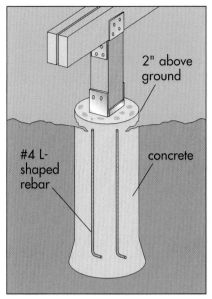

Reinforce footings with rebar.
Reinforcing steel bars, or rebar, add strength to concrete structures. Building codes generally stipulate the number and size of rebar needed. Deck piers typically need one or two pieces of rebar set in the concrete.

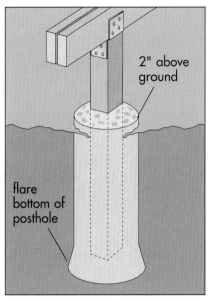

Embed the post in concrete.
Pressure-treated posts can be embedded in concrete piers, eliminating the need for metal post anchors. This technique creates a stronger foundation than other methods, but aligning the posts is trickier. Also, moisture may accumulate between the post and the concrete, creating a place that may eventually weaken with rot.

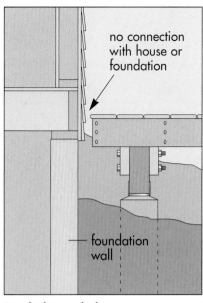

Let deck stand alone.
A freestanding deck has no connection with the house. The ledger, which is bolted to the house, is replaced by an extra row of posts and another beam. This method eliminates the danger of weather-induced damage to the house due to improper flashing.

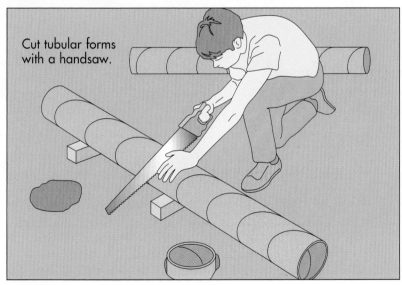

Use fiber-form tubes.
Fiber-form tubes are an easy way to make concrete piers. They may be required by codes in areas where loose or sandy soils are common. The tubes are sold in 12-foot lengths, in various widths. The tubes should be cut as square as possible with a handsaw, then suspended above the bottom of the hole (see page 43) to allow concrete to spread out and form a wider footing.

EXPERTS' INSIGHT

WORKING WITH CONCRETE

Too much water weakens concrete. When properly mixed, the concrete will be wet enough to pour, yet dry enough to hold its shape when formed into small ridges. Pour concrete mix into a watertight tub. Form a crater in the center, then add water gradually from a bucket as you mix. Concrete can irritate your skin; wear gloves and long sleeves when mixing it.

DRAWING PLANS

You don't need a drafting or architectural degree to produce accurate plan drawings of your deck. But you may need drawn plans to obtain a building permit. Don't be surprised if you are required to have an architect's stamped approval on the plans. Use graph paper to draw elevation and overhead views of your deck to scale (typically ¼ inch to the foot). Drawing working plans can be tedious, but the work pays off by eliminating all of the guesswork from construction. Add enlarged detail or section drawings of railings, stairs, and other complex components that can't be presented in specific detail on the main drawings.

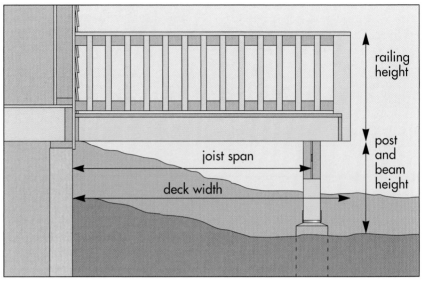

Draw elevation (side or front) view.
An elevation drawing is a vertical view of the deck. It should include each layer of the deck, from footings to railings, with appropriate dimensions given for each. In addition to a side elevation view, you might find it helpful to draw a front elevation, which would be the view if you were looking directly at the house.

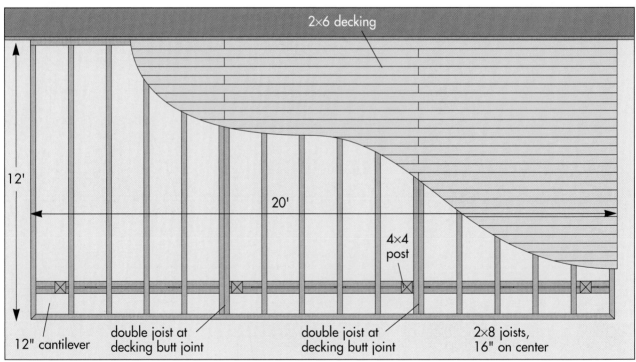

Complete a plan view.
Also called a bird's-eye or overhead view, a plan view shows the footprint of the deck. It is particularly important in establishing exact locations for piers, beams, and joists. An accurately scaled plan view not only helps guide the framing of the deck, it allows you to estimate the amount of lumber to buy. The drawing above combines a view of the finished deck with the decking installed and the foundation and framing. On more complex decks, these two perspectives can be drawn separately. Draw the foundation and framing plan first, then use tracing paper to produce the finished view.

ORDERING AND STORING LUMBER

With your plans drawn, you can write up a list of the lumber and other materials you'll need to complete the project. The list at *right* shows the required lengths for most of the lumber for a typical 12×20-foot deck. Because lumber generally is sold in lengths of even-numbered feet (beginning with 8 feet), however, your final lumber order will be different.

Plan your order for the most efficient use of lumber. For example, the decking requires two boards to complete each run. You could buy a 14–foot board and an 8–foot board for each run, but you'll have less waste if you buy all 14-foot boards and cut some of them in half. Allow at least 10 percent for waste.

With the lumber and materials list, shop around for the best prices and delivery fees. Be sure to find out if you will be able to return unused lumber.

Plan for outside lumber storage
Store wood outside by "stickering" it with strips of wood in between layers to create air spaces. Use scrap pieces of 2×4s or 4×4s to keep the stack off the ground. Weights on top of the stack help prevent warping. Cover the stack with a tarp.

LUMBER AND MATERIALS LIST FOR 12×20-FOOT BASIC DECK

Foundation (for 3-foot frost line)

Premixed concrete		4⅔ cubic feet
Fiber-form tubes	4	8×38"
Gravel or sand		as needed for drainage
Rebar	8	No.4 L-shaped pieces

Framing

Ledger board	1	2×8×10'
	1	2×8×9'9"
Metal flashing		as needed
Posts	4	4×4× needed deck height
Beams	2	2×10×13'
	2	2×10×7'
Plywood spacers (for beams)	11	½×3×8"
Joists	16	2×8×11'9"
End joists	2	2×8×12'
Header joists	1	2×8×6'6"
	1	2×8×13'3"

Decking

Decking boards	39	2×6×14'

Nails and Fasteners

Joist hangers	12	2×8
	2	3½×8
Post anchors	4	4×4
Post caps	4	4×4
Bolts or anchors for ledger		as needed
16d common nails or 3-inch decking screws @1,000/lb		about 14 pounds

Optional

Stairs	
Railings	
Sealer/stain	

INSTALLING THE LEDGER

The ledger attaches to the house framing or a masonry wall. It serves the same function as a beam, except that the load carried by the ledger is transferred to the house foundation. Installing a ledger first creates a reference point for the rest of your deck. Using a ledger reduces costs and labor by cutting the number of postholes that must be dug and filled with concrete.

However, attaching the ledger can be a time-consuming chore—one of the most difficult steps in building a deck. On houses with beveled siding, you may need to cut away some siding to create a flat surface for the ledger. This opening must then be flashed carefully to keep water out of the wall. The ledger should be of the same dimension lumber as the joists and 3 inches shorter than the width of the deck to allow room for the overlapping end joists.

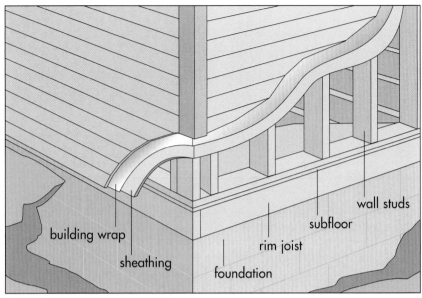

Locate the ledger on the house.
The finished deck surface should sit about 1 inch below the bottom of any door threshold. Add this figure to the thickness of the decking material to determine the location for the top of the ledger.

Thus, if you are using 2×6 decking (1½ inches thick), measure 2½ inches below the bottom of the threshold, then draw a level line at this height to represent the top of the ledger.

Attach ledger to masonry wall, ...
Cut the ledger to size and have a helper hold it in place against the wall. Make sure the ledger is level, then drill bolt holes through the ledger every 16 inches. Insert a pencil through the holes to mark their

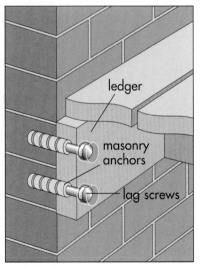

location on the wall. Remove the ledger and drill holes for expansion anchors at the marked locations. Insert the anchors, then attach the ledger by inserting lag screws, with a washer, through the ledger and tightening them.

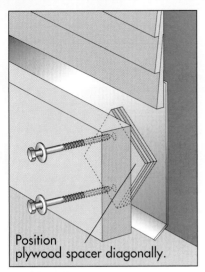

Position plywood spacer diagonally.

attach with spacers, ...

An air space between the ledger and the wall helps keep both dry. Your building supplier may stock plastic or aluminum spacers manufactured for deck use, but you easily can cut your own out of pressure-treated plywood. Position the spacer

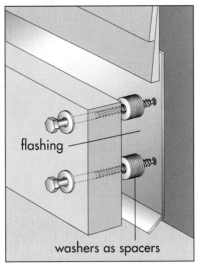

flashing

washers as spacers

diagonally so it sheds water. Other choices for spacers include galvanized or stainless steel washers or sections of plastic or metal pipe cut to length. If you use pipe, add washers on either end to keep the pipe from digging into the ledger and flashing.

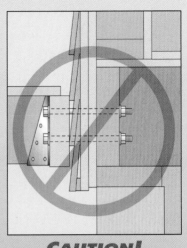

CAUTION!
DON'T ATTACH THE LEDGER TO THE SIDING
You're asking for trouble if you attach the ledger directly to clapboard or beveled siding, as shown above. First, you create a pocket for water. Second, tightening the ledger against the uneven surface crushes the siding. Both consequences can undermine the connection and lead to serious water damage.

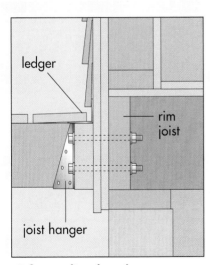

ledger

rim joist

joist hanger

or fasten directly to house.

This section view shows a ledger properly installed on a clapboard wall. The siding has been removed and flashing added to keep water out of the house. The ledger is bolted through the rim joist.

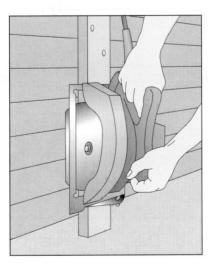

To make even, vertical cuts through uneven siding, use a 2×4 as a flat surface for the saw. Set the blade just deep enough to remove the siding without cutting into the sheathing.

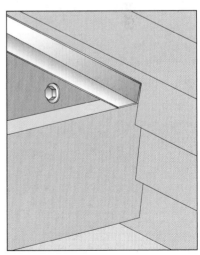

Slide the flashing under the siding an inch or more (cut a notch around the door threshold if necessary). After the ledger and joists have been installed, bend the flashing over the ledger edge to allow water to drip off.

PREPARING THE SITE

Eliminate drainage problems around your proposed deck before you build it. Some of the ground beneath the deck will be wet from time to time, but you want the areas around the foundation to be firm. If you have standing water or chronic soggy areas near the site, consult a landscaping contractor for advice on improving the drainage. If a downspout empties close to the deck, reroute it. If necessary, add a drainage ditch to divert water away from the house and deck. Be sure water drains into a dry well or municipal sewer and not into a neighbor's yard.

gravel

landscaping fabric

batter board

YOU'LL NEED

TIME: Several hours to remove the sod; about 2 hours for simple grading and spreading gravel.
SKILLS: No special skills, although removing sod can be hard work.
TOOLS: Garden rake, flat garden spade.

1. Level the grade.
Install batter boards and pound stakes in place for tying guidelines to aid you in grading the site. (You'll set guidelines for the deck structure later.) Remove the sod. If the deck will be close to the ground, check for high spots in the grade that could interfere with joist placement. Smooth high spots with a rake or shovel. To

ensure grass and weeds won't grow under the deck, cover the area with landscaping fabric. In addition to controlling weeds, landscaping fabric allows water to drain through it while keeping the gravel from sinking into the soil. Fasten the fabric in place with landscaping fabric staples and cover the surface with a 2- to 3-inch layer of gravel.

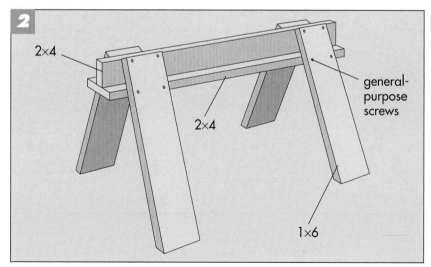

2×4

2×4

general-purpose screws

1×6

2. Build sawhorses.
You'll need a stable work platform on which to cut your deck material. This sawhorse design is easy to build and far more sturdy than the metal-bracket and scrap-

lumber types you can buy at home centers. Cut one 8-foot 2×4 in half to make the T-beam. Make the 30-inch legs from a single 10-foot 1×6. Put it together with 2½-inch general-purpose screws.

EXPERTS' INSIGHT

PLAN FOR LUMBER

Give some thought to where to unload and store the lumber. Store the lumber close enough to the deck site to save you from moving it again, but not so close that it interferes with construction. A garage near the deck site is ideal for keeping lumber dry and secure. If you store lumber outdoors for any length of time, see the recommendations on page 35.

LAYING OUT A DECK

After installing the ledger and preparing the ground, lay out the structural elements of your deck. Layout is the process of marking the perimeter of the deck with mason's lines so you can establish the location of postholes. It is not physically demanding work, but the success of your project depends on locating the lines accurately.

The main reason for installing the ledger on the house first (see pages 36–37) is to create a solid and level reference point for creating an accurate layout. The mason's lines marking the perimeter of the deck should be level. If you are building a deck on a sloped site, you need to make the stakes for the batter boards long enough to allow for a level line. If you allow the mason's line to run parallel with the slope, the dimensions for your deck will be thrown off, perhaps by a significant margin.

The illustration below shows both the site layout and the relationship of the layout to the finished deck itself. The mason's lines running perpendicular to the ledger mark the outside faces of the end joists. The line running parallel with the ledger helps locate the centers of the foundation piers.

On a more complicated deck, you might want to set up one set of mason's lines to mark the perimeter of the deck and another to locate postholes. (Use different colored string to identify each.)

Finally, decide where you want to set up a work site and where you will pile lumber scraps. Create a temporary worktable by laying a couple of 2×4s and a piece of plywood on sawhorses. Make sure you have extension cords long enough to reach your work site from the nearest outlet.

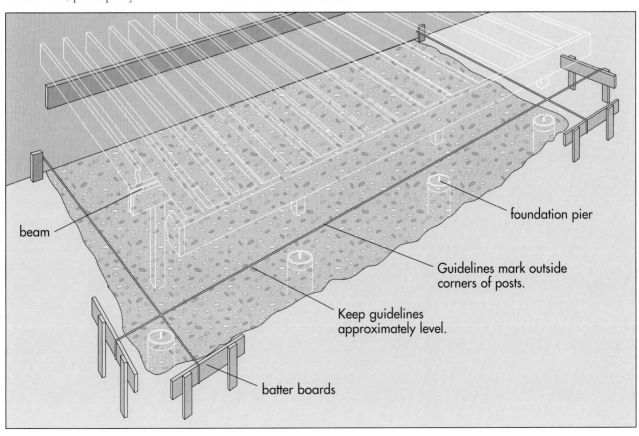

beam

foundation pier

Guidelines mark outside corners of posts.

Keep guidelines approximately level.

batter boards

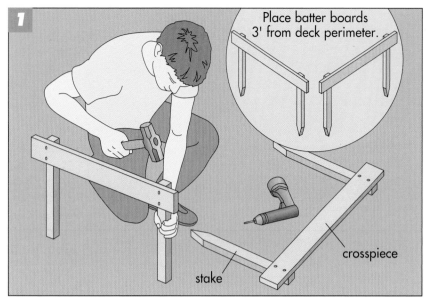

Place batter boards 3' from deck perimeter.

crosspiece

stake

1. Build batter boards.

To lay out a basic rectangular deck, build two pairs of batter boards. Use 1×4s or 2×4s for the stakes and crosspieces. Stakes should be 3- to 4-feet long if the site is level, longer if it's sloping. You can buy pointed stakes at the lumberyard or cut points on the bottoms of the stakes yourself. Cut the crosspiece to length and attach it to the stakes with screws or nails. Locate the stakes about 3 feet away from where the mason's lines will intersect and drive the stakes straight into the ground with a baby sledgehammer. Drive the stakes deep enough to support tightly stretched lines. You'll position the top of the crosspiece level with the top of the ledger when you level the mason's lines.

SQUARING UP WITH THE 3–4–5 METHOD

If you don't get your deck lay-out square, it will create problems at every succeeding step. Mason's lines that are out of square result in postholes in the wrong spots. Misaligned post-holes lead to sloppy post configurations and cockeyed beams. To ensure that your lay-out is square, use the 3–4–5 method, illustrated below. Multiples of these dimensions, such as 6–8–10 or 9–12–15, are even more accurate. From a corner, measure 3 feet along the back edge and 4 feet along the other edge, marking the spots with a piece of tape. Make sure both of these measurements begin at exactly the same point. If the layout is square, the diagonal measurement between the marks will be 5 feet. If it isn't, adjust the mason's line until the diagonal measures up.

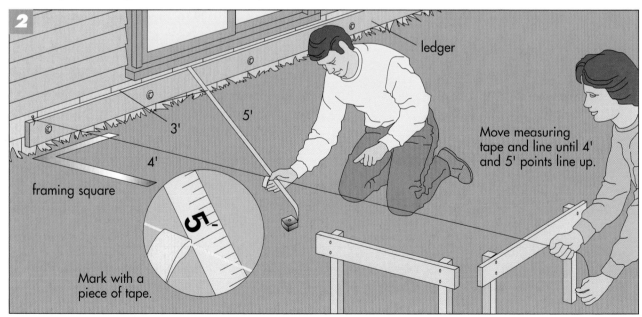

ledger

5'

3'

4'

framing square

Move measuring tape and line until 4' and 5' points line up.

Mark with a piece of tape.

2. Position string lines.

Adjusting the mason's lines is best done with two people. Drive a nail into the top side of the ledger, 1½ inches in from the edge. Tie a line to the nailhead and stretch it past the batter board. Use a framing square to roughly position the line perpendicular with the face of the ledger. Then tape the line to the batter board crosspiece. Repeat the process at the other end of the ledger. Next, measure along each mason's line to locate the centerline of the footings. For our 12×20-foot deck this will be 11 feet from the back of the ledger. Mark the location on the line with tape, then run another line parallel to the ledger, intersecting the 11-foot marks.

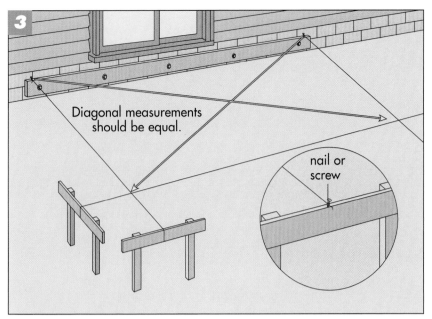

3

Diagonal measurements should be equal.

nail or screw

3. Check your layout.

With a helper, carefully measure the diagonals inside the mason's lines. If they are equal, the layout is square. If they are not equal, adjust the taped line ends until they are. Once you are sure the lines are square, drive nails or screws into the tops of the crosspieces at the proper location. Leave the nail or screw sticking out about an inch and tie the line around it snugly. If you bump the batter boards at any point, check for square again and readjust the mason's lines as needed.

EXPERTS' INSIGHT

CHECK AND CHECK AGAIN

With the mason's lines in place and the posthole locations marked, check your layout one more time before you start digging. Sometimes batter boards can settle or shift. Or perhaps they tilted out of square when you pounded the nail in for the mason's line.

Take a few moments to measure from the ledger out to the center of each posthole location to ensure they are the same distance. Also, check to be sure the distance between each of the posthole locations is consistent.

4

6"

mason's line 11' from ledger

plumb bob

4. Locate postholes.

This is another job that may be done more easily with two people. On our basic deck, the outside footings will be centered 6 inches from the sides of the deck. On the 11-foot mason's line, measure in 6 inches from each side string line. Using a dark permanent marker, mark the mason's line. From each of those marks, measure in another 6 feet 4 inches to locate the two intermediate postholes and mark the mason's line again. To transfer the marks on the mason's line to the ground, use a plumb bob.

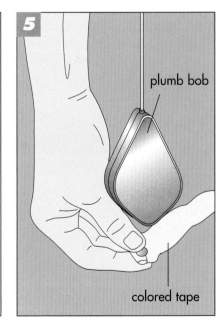

5

plumb bob

colored tape

5. Mark posthole locations.

Dangle the plumb bob just above ground level. When it is perfectly still, mark the location by sticking a large nail directly under it. For added visibility, first pierce the nail through a piece of colored tape or paper. The nail marks the center of each posthole.

DIGGING POSTHOLES

Before you dig postholes, check with your local building department for specific code requirements for the type, depth, and strength of deck posts and footings. These codes are based on local climate and terrain. Footings must be stable in soft soil, withstand frost heave, and provide a base to keep posts or beams above decay-causing moisture.

The depth for post footings should be below the frostline (the depth to which frost permeates the soil) to prevent movement caused by freezing and thawing. This depth varies with local climate. You may be required to place a precast pier pad on gravel below the frostline.

A posthole normally is between 24 and 42 inches deep, depending upon the soil type, the depth to the frostline, and the height of the post. If the soil at the base of the hole seems loose, compact it with a tamper. Don't try to dig postholes with a shovel; at the least you should borrow, rent, or buy a posthole digger. If your design requires a large number of holes, rent a power auger (see page 26) or hire a contractor to handle the job. If you rent a power auger, be sure to get thorough instructions on its use.

YOU'LL NEED

TIME: 1 to 4 hours, depending on the type of tool used to dig the holes, the type of soil, and the number and depth of the holes.
SKILLS: Using a manual posthole digger requires no special skills, but get complete instructions before using a power auger.
TOOLS: Garden spade, clamshell posthole digger, digging bar, sheet of plywood or plastic.

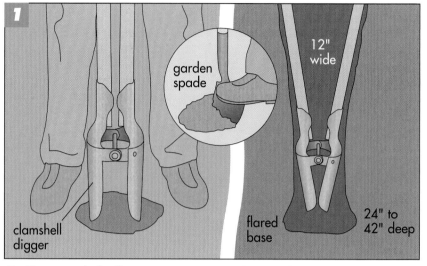

1. Use a posthole digger.
If needed, use a garden spade to remove sod. With the handles squeezed together, jam the posthole digger into the ground. Spread the handles apart and lift the dirt out. If you hit large rocks, rent or buy a digging bar (basically an elongated crowbar). Roots can be cut with a tree saw. Do your best to keep the hole as plumb as possible and the bottom level. Flare the bottom of the hole to widen the footing base. Holes should be about 12 inches wide for a typical 4×4 post.

2. Keep dirt away from hole.
If you have never dug a posthole, you may be surprised at how much dirt is removed. Don't make the mistake of piling dirt too close to the hole. Set it several feet away, preferably on a sheet of plywood or plastic to make your clean-up job simple.

CAUTION!
TAKE YOUR TIME
Digging postholes is demanding labor. If you need to dig holes that are 3 to 4 feet deep, do not be surprised if you spend up to an hour on some holes. You may spend a good bit of this time coaxing out rocks and cutting through roots. This work can be tough on the arms and shoulders and even tougher on the back. Even if you are in relatively good physical shape, it makes sense to take your time and take frequent breaks. As hard as the digging is, don't cheat on the required depth. Rest assured that once this task is finished the rest of the job will seem easy.

PREPARING THE FOUNDATION

If you removed the mason's lines to dig the postholes, carefully replace them. Make sure the postholes are deep and wide enough for the footings required for your deck. Remember, the base of the footings must be below the frostline. If the site gets lots of moisture, place gravel in the holes to aid drainage. Cut fiber-form tubes with a handsaw, taking care to make square cuts. These forms should be long enough so they are at least 2 inches above grade and about 6 inches above the bottom of the hole.

YOU'LL NEED

TIME: 1 to 2 hours for each posthole, including building the forms, mixing and pouring the concrete, and inserting the post base.
SKILLS: Basic masonry skills; follow instructions on the bag to mix concrete.
TOOLS: Mixing tub, mason's hoe, shovel, water hose.

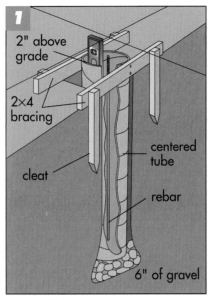

2" above grade
2×4 bracing
cleat
centered tube
rebar
6" of gravel

1. Build the forms.
Set a fiber-form tube into each hole and fasten 2×4 braces to the sides with decking screws. Center the tube under the mason's line and check for plumb. Drive short cleats into the ground and attach them to the braces. Cut a piece of rebar to length and place it in each tube. Fill each tube with a foot of concrete. After a few minutes, lift the rebar 4 inches off the bottom.

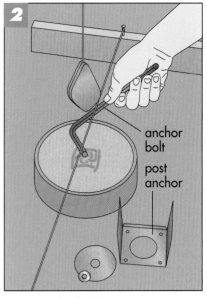

anchor bolt
post anchor

2. Pour the footings.
Fill the remainder of the tube with concrete. Before the concrete sets, insert an anchor bolt into the center of the footing. Leave the threaded end protruding upward with the shank perpendicular to the footing surface. Smooth the surface of the concrete. After the concrete is set, the post anchor can be positioned on the bolt.

ESTIMATING CONCRETE NEEDS

■ Whether you mix concrete yourself or have ready-mix concrete delivered by truck, you need to know in advance how much you will need. Most ready-mix companies require a minimum order, which you may be able to meet only if you are building a large deck requiring many postholes.
■ To make your own concrete, you can buy premixed bags weighing up to 90 pounds each. These generally make from $\frac{1}{3}$ to $\frac{2}{3}$ cubic foot per bag, but check the label to determine how much mixed concrete can be made from each bag.

■ To calculate how much concrete you need, determine how much is required for each hole, then multiply that amount by the number of holes. Calculate the total volume of each hole using this formula: 3.14 times the squared radius (one-half the diameter) times the height (total depth of the posthole). A 1-foot diameter hole, 3.5 feet deep, would require 3.14 square feet of concrete. (3.14 x .5^2 x 3.5 = 2.75)
■ If you set the posts in the concrete footing, subtract the space that the post will fill in each hole to determine accurately the amount of concrete needed.

Money $ Saver

PREPARE STAIR LANDING
If you plan to rest stairs on a concrete pad, you may be able to save time and energy by preparing the pad now so you can complete your concrete work at one time.

The trick is determining exactly where the pad will be placed, which is difficult to gauge when the deck hasn't been built yet. To position the pad accurately you have to trust your plans and know where you want the stairs located. See page 56 for positioning and building a form for pouring a concrete stair landing.

INSTALLING POSTS

Before installing the posts, you'll need to remove the mason's line centered over the footings. Before doing so, however, you might want to add another line to help you to align the posts. For 4×4 posts, set this line 1¾ inches (half the actual width of a 4×4) from the existing line. Then, set the posts in place with the face of the post just touching the newly placed line.

YOU'LL NEED

TIME: About 20 to 30 minutes to install each post.
SKILLS: The ability to establish plumb using a level.
TOOLS: Hammer, cordless drill or screwdriver, level.

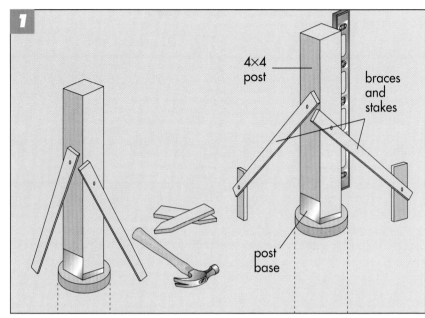

1. Set and brace the posts.
Measure and cut the posts so they are higher than the bottom of the ledger. For each post, you'll need two stakes and two braces. Insert the post into the post anchor. Hold it as straight as possible and attach the braces with one screw so they pivot. Drive the stakes into the ground next to each brace. Using a level, plumb two adjacent sides of each post. Holding the post plumb, have a helper attach the braces to the stakes.

EXPERTS' INSIGHT

CUT YOUR POSTS DOWN TO SIZE

Always rough-cut posts longer than actually needed. With the post braced in place, the extra length allows you to plumb it easily. This is important if you are building a low deck whose posts might finally be only 1 or 2 feet high. Also, the extra length provides you with some working space for transferring the ledger height to the post and measuring down the post to the proper post height. Once you have double-checked your marks, detach the post from the bracing and cut it to the proper length, or cut in place.

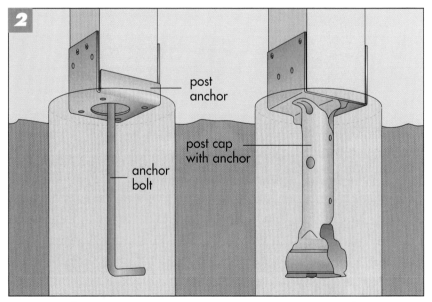

2. Fasten the posts.
Before attaching the post to the post anchor, recheck the post for plumb. When the post is plumb, drive nails or screws through the anchor into the post. Post anchors and caps vary, so be sure to use the type and number of fasteners specified by the manufacturer. Take care when driving fasteners that you don't move the post out of alignment. When finished, recheck the post for plumb. Finally, use a utility knife to cut away any of the fiber-form tube that remains above ground level.

MARKING AND CUTTING POSTS

Marking and cutting posts is a relatively delicate operation. If you get it right, your deck will be level and the rest of the job will be easier. Get it wrong, and you'll mar the appearance and actually complicate later steps. So don't rush this step. Enlist an assistant if possible to help with transferring level marks. If time has passed since you set your posts, check them for plumb. Often, posts get bumped or bracing gets kicked, knocking your supports out of plumb. Readjust if necessary.

YOU'LL NEED

TIME: About 15 minutes per post.
SKILLS: Ability to use a level, cut upright posts with a circular saw.
TOOLS: A long straight board, carpenter's level or water level, pencil, tape measure tape, circular saw, chisel.

CAUTION!
TREATING CUT POSTS

If you are using pressure-treated lumber for your deck, have a supply of wood preservative on hand. Although the treated wood absorbs a good dose of the chemicals used in preserving the wood, the coverage is most thorough on the outer surfaces. When you cut a treated post or board, you expose wood that is less-thoroughly treated. To avoid future maintenance problems with your deck, brush some preservative on the cut ends. Because they'll be most exposed to weather, horizontal surfaces, such as posts ends, particularly need this treatment.

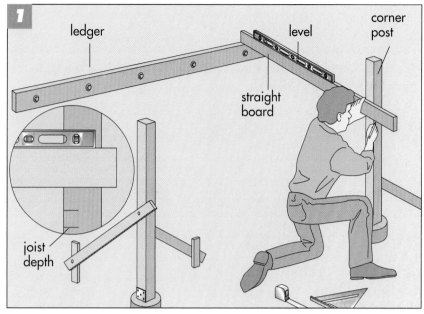

1. Establish post height.
Rest one end of a long straight board on top of the ledger. Hold the other end against a corner post. Place a level on top of the board and level it. Mark where the bottom of the board touches the post. Next, measure down from that mark the depth of a joist. (For a 2×8 joist, measure down 7¼ inches.) Measure down from this second mark the depth of the beam (for a 10-inch beam, this would be 9¼ inches). Make a level mark at this location around the post. This is the post cutoff line.

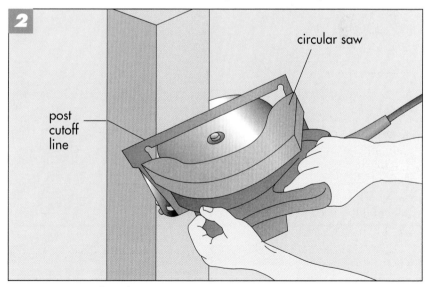

2. Cut posts to length.
After the cutoff lines are marked on each post, double-check your measurements by placing a long board and level along the line of posts. Make sure the cutoff lines are level with each other. Set your circular saw for a maximum depth of cut, then cut from opposite sides of each post, taking care to follow the lines. If you have trouble making level cuts, tack a board across the posts to rest the baseplate of the saw on. If necessary, use a sharp chisel to clean off the post top.

INSTALLING THE BEAM

On our basic deck design, the beam sits on top of the posts, and joists sit on top of the beam. Joists also can be set on the same plane as the beam by installing them with joist hangers.

The beam should be pressure-treated unless you are using a naturally rot-resistant wood. Sometimes it is difficult to find a solid 4× beam in the width you need, and a 4×10 or 4×12 beam can be heavy. For these reasons, a built-up beam made of two 2×s can be more convenient.

To ensure the outside edges of the beam align squarely with the ledger, reattach the mason's lines marking the sides of the deck before installing the beam. This is far more important than having the ends of the beam overhang the outside posts by the same distance. Check for square and measure the diagonals from beam to ledger before fastening the beam to the posts.

Generally, beams should be installed with the crown side up. To find the crown, sight down the narrow edges of a board (see *page 49*). If one edge seems to have a high spot (crown) on it, place a mark on this edge to remind you to set this edge up. In constructing a built-up beam, make sure the crowns of both boards are on the same side of the beam.

YOU'LL NEED

TIME: About 1 hour for a solid beam; longer if installing a built-up beam.
SKILLS: Cutting large-dimension lumber, fastening.
TOOLS: Hammer, circular saw, drill and bits, wrench, level.

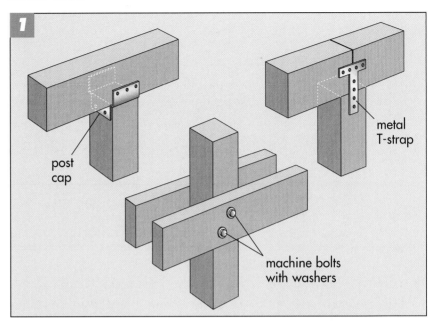

post cap

metal T-strap

machine bolts with washers

1. Join beam to posts.
The beam-to-post connection is critical to the integrity of your deck. The strongest connections are formed when the beam rests fully on top of the posts, as with the top two examples above. Metal brackets, straps, or ties add additional stability. You'll be able to select from a wide variety of these fasteners at your home center or lumberyard. Your building supplier should be able to help you choose the right one for your deck. With these connectors, always use the type and number of nails or screws recommended by the manufacturer.

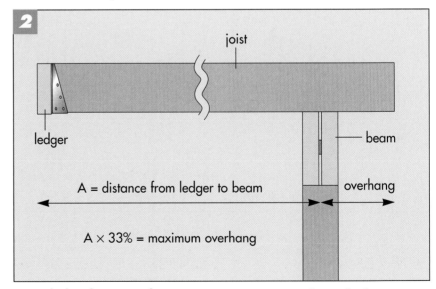

joist

ledger

beam

A = distance from ledger to beam

overhang

A × 33% = maximum overhang

2. Calculate beam overhang.
On our basic deck design, the posts are centered 11 feet from the house, while the deck surface extends to 12 feet. This overhang, or cantilever, creates a more attractive deck because the beam is set back out of view. In general, joists can overhang the beam one-third, or about 33 percent, of the distance between the ledger and the beam. However, your local building code may dictate different requirements: Be sure to check on cantilever limits.

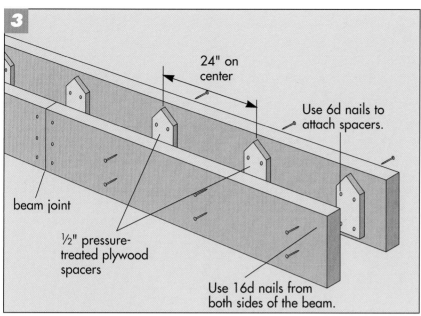

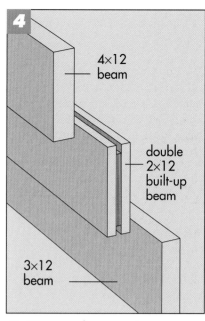

3. Construct a built-up beam.

A beam composed of two 2× boards separated by ½-inch spacers will match the width of 4×4 posts. The spacers also allow water to drain through the boards, ensuring a longer life than if they were nailed together. Use pressure-treated plywood to make the spacers, and point the tips to encourage water runoff. Use a spacer every 24 inches on center. Attach the spacers with 6d galvanized nails and drive 16d galvanized nails through the beam and spacers from both sides of the beam. Stagger joints and place them over posts.

4. Size up a beam.

If you make a built-up beam using two 2× boards, keep in mind that the structural strength of the beam is not equal to a 4× beam. It is only equal to the width of the two boards (3 inches), not its finished width (3½ inches). Spacers don't add strength.

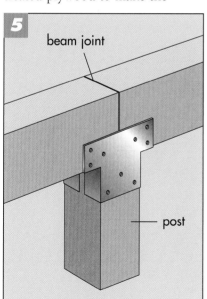

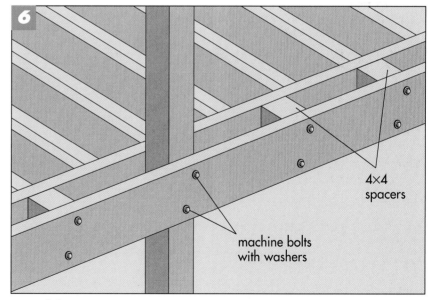

5. Place joints over posts.

For a built-up beam, it is smart to locate even staggered joints over a post. If you are using a solid beam, however, you must center all joints over posts. Cut the beam squarely so as much of the beam as possible contacts the post.

6. Bolt beams to continuous posts.

If your deck has posts running through the framing for railings, you should bolt a double beam to the posts as shown above. Use short pieces of 4×4 as spacers and use ½-inch machine bolts with washers on both sides. To reduce the chance of splitting a post, offset the bolts horizontally. Note that this technique relies on the fasteners for much of its strength and integrity. It is not as strong as when the beam sits on top of the posts. It is a good idea to consult with a building professional before using this approach.

HANGING JOISTS

If properly installed, joist hangers are a more secure method of attaching joists to the ledger than the old technique of toenailing joists. In fact, most building codes require hangers for deck joists. Take care to buy joist hangers that match the size of joist you are installing. A 2×6 joist requires a different hanger than a 2×8 joist. Make sure the hangers are intended for exterior use. For built-up or 4× joists, use 3½-inch-wide hangers. For end joists, use a heavy-duty right-angle bracket. This attaches on the inside corner so no hardware is visible.

YOU'LL NEED

TIME: 15 to 20 minutes to mark and fasten each joist.
SKILLS: Measuring, cutting, installing joist hangers.
TOOLS: Hammer, tape measure, pencil, framing square, speed square, circular saw.

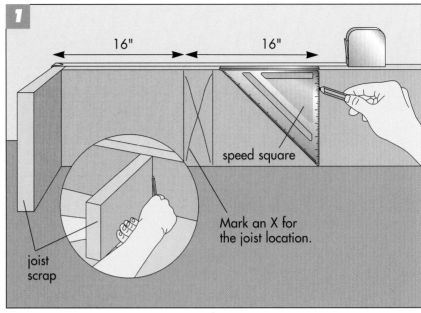

1. Lay out joists on the ledger.
Temporarily tack a scrap piece of 2× joist stock to the end of the ledger to represent the end joist you will install later. Hook your tape over the edge of this scrap and make a mark every 16 inches on the front edge of the ledger.

Then go back with a square and extend each mark down the face of the ledger. Use a scrap of joist stock set on the joist side of each line to mark the width of each joist. Mark an X between the two lines to make it clear where each joist should go.

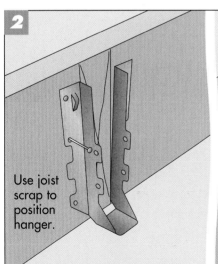

2. Attach joist hangers.
Attaching a joist hanger can be trickier than it looks. Use the fasteners recommended by the joist manufacturer. Hold the hanger with one side aligned with the layout mark on the ledger.

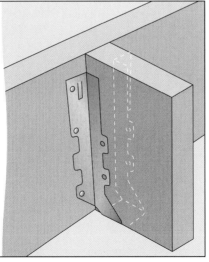

Use a scrap piece of joist stock to make sure the hanger is positioned so the joist top and ledger top are flush. Nail one side of the hanger to the ledger, leaving the other side loose.

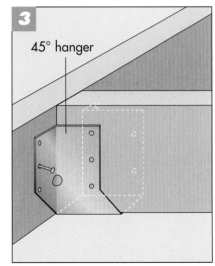

3. Use special hangers for angles.
Some deck designs have joists that meet the ledger at an angle. Forty-five degree hangers usually can handle a 40- to 50-degree angle. Use bendable seismic anchors for other angles. Cut joist ends at the appropriate angle for full bearing.

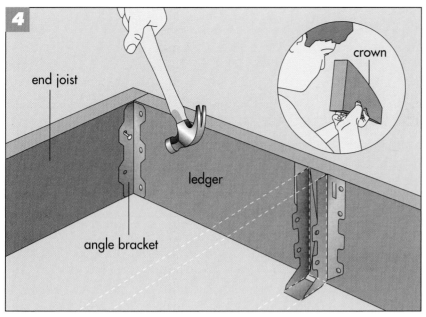

4. Install the joists.

Measure and cut the joists to length. Both ends should be square and free of splits. The end joists will be 1½ inches longer than the others to overlap the ledger. Apply preservative to the cut ends. Set each joist in place

with the crown up (see inset). Make sure joists are straight and parallel. Nail in the other side of the hanger, then nail joists to the hangers. Overlap the end joists on the ledger ends, then attach angle brackets to the inside corner.

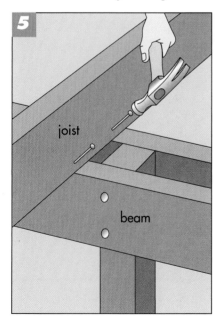

5. Attach joists to beam.

With the joists straight and square with the ledger, fasten each with a 16d nail driven at an angle into the beam just deep enough to hold it in place. (After installing the header joist, you can remove these nails to allow the frame to be squared up.)

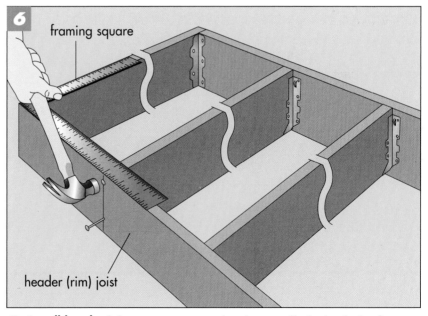

6. Install header joist.

The header, or rim, joist is fastened to the ends of the joists. It's helpful to mark a layout on the header similar to that on the ledger. While a helper aligns the tops, drive three 16d nails through the header into the joist. With the

header installed, check the frame for square by measuring the diagonals. If necessary, remove the toenails at the beam to make minor adjustments. Finally, fasten joists to the beam permanently with two 16d nails toenailed through each side of the joist.

INSTALLING DECK BOARDS

Don't cut corners when it comes to choosing your decking material. This surface is the business side of your deck. It gets the most use and takes the most abuse. If your lumber and decking were not pretreated, consider applying a water repellent now. At this point, you can coat the tops of the joists and reach other parts of the deck that may be inaccessible later. It's also a good idea to coat both sides of the deck boards before installing them.

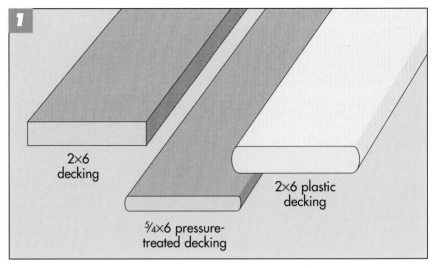

YOU'LL NEED

TIME: One-half to a full day for a basic deck, depending on material and design.
SKILLS: Cutting and fastening boards straight and secure.
TOOLS: Circular saw, hammer or screw gun or drill equipped to drive screws, chalk line or mason's line.

1. Choose your decking.
Building centers generally carry several choices of material for decking. Nominal 6-inch boards are the most popular width. Boards wider than 6 inches tend to warp too much, while narrower boards take longer to install. Standard 2×6 boards are 1½ inches thick and are the least expensive. Five quarter (⁵⁄₄ inch)

boards are about 1 inch thick and cost a little more. However, they are often a better grade of wood and are available with a radius edge (rounded edge). Decking also is available in plastic and wood-plastic composites. The process for installation is the same as wood decking. These products cost more, but they require little long-term maintenance.

2. Select deck board fasteners.
Several products now are available to fasten deck boards to joists without nailing or screwing through the surface of the decking. These fasteners are concealed between boards. That means a better-looking deck and less rotting around fasteners. These fasteners, however, make it more difficult to remove and replace individual boards at a later date. They also cost more than nails or screws and installation is more time-consuming. You may not be able to find all the options shown here at your home center, but one or two should be available.

Galvanized or anodized deck screws (see page 31) hold the best and are relatively quick to install. Galvanized nails (see page 31) are faster to install, particularly if you use a pneumatic nailer (see page 27), but can pop out over time.

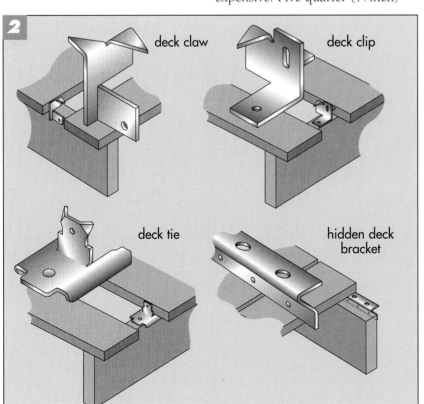

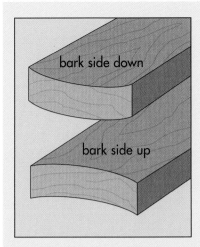

WHICH SIDE UP?

A rule of thumb is to install decking boards with the bark side up. It is thought this allows water to drain off if the board cups. However, studies show decking installed with the bark side down is less likely to develop splits in the surface. The best advice is to make sure the wood is dry and install the best looking side up. For added prevention, apply water repellent every year.

EXPERTS' INSIGHT

SCATTER THE BOARDS

Making a trip to your lumber pile every time you need another decking board wastes time and energy. Instead, carry a number of decking boards to the deck and scatter them across the joists.

As you begin laying the decking, you can use the loose boards as a working platform, particularly when you are right up against the house. Later, you can position your reserve boards so each can be pulled quickly into place for fastening.

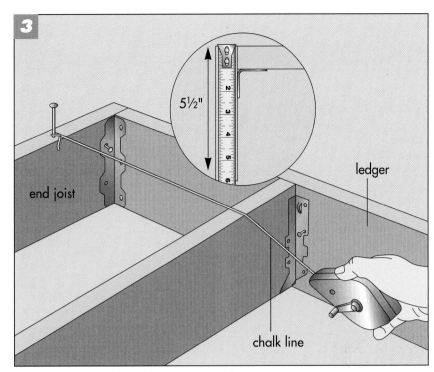

3. Install starter board.

Your job will proceed much easier if you install the first board as straight and as square as possible. On both end joists, measure out from the house the width of one decking board (5½ inches) plus ¼ inch for a drainage gap. Mark the joists, then snap a chalk line or run a mason's line between them. Set the first decking board along this line. For best results, use the straightest board you can find for the starter board.

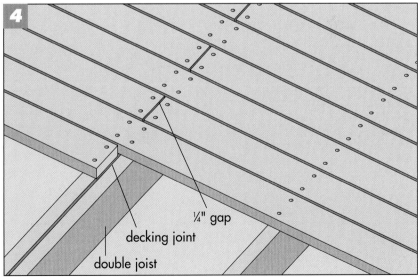

4. Stagger joints.

On a narrow deck, you may not have any butt joints between decking boards. However, on our 20-foot-wide basic deck, we planned for the joints by installing two sets of double joists. This requires the use of one long and one short board in each row of decking, with the joints staggered on the double joists. Leave a ¼-inch gap between board ends to allow for water drainage through the decking and the double joist.

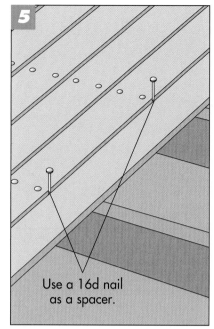

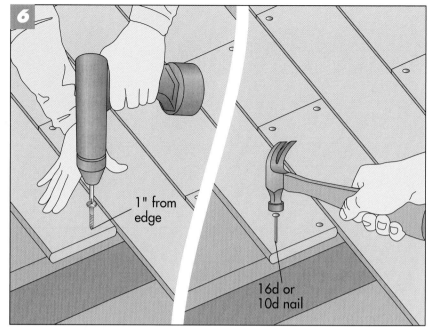

Use a 16d nail as a spacer.

1" from edge

16d or 10d nail

5. Leave a space between boards.

Deck boards need to have a gap between them to allow water and dirt to fall through. Bear in mind that the wood shrinks over time as it continues to dry. Use a 16d common nail as a spacer.

6. Use proper fastening methods.

Decking can be installed with decking screws, nails (16d nails for 2× decking, 10d nails for ⁵⁄4 decking), or special concealed fasteners. Use two nails or screws at each joist crossing, about 1 inch from each side of the board. Whether using nails or screws,

drill angled pilot holes at the ends of boards to prevent splits. Drive heads of nails flush with the decking. As the wood dries, drive them deeper. If you use a pneumatic nailer (see page 27), adjust the depth so the nail heads are slightly below the surface of the decking board.

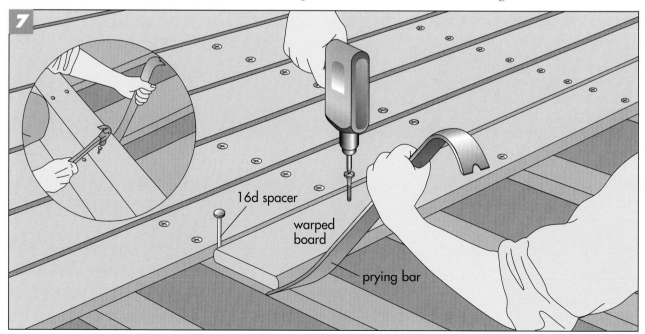

16d spacer

warped board

prying bar

7. Keep it straight.

Straighten crooked boards as you fasten them. Use a utility-grade chisel or a pry bar to force warped boards into alignment. You can do this by yourself (see inset), but the

process is much simpler if you lever the decking while a helper drives in the fasteners. On severely warped boards, you may have to repeat this from one joist to the next. Check for straightness every

few rows by measuring from the header joist. If you're significantly out of true, hide the mistake by making small adjustments in the spacing gap over several of the next rows rather than all at once.

EXPERTS' INSIGHT

PLANNING AN OVERHANG

Give some thought to the amount of overhang you want on your finished deck. An overhang isn't necessary. You can cut the decking flush with the joists. However, you may be happier with the appearance of your deck if you let the decking extend beyond the edges on each side.

A 1- to 2-inch overhang is most common and gives a finished appearance to your deck. As you install your decking, let the boards overhang the end joists (see below). They will be cut to length after the entire decking surface is installed.

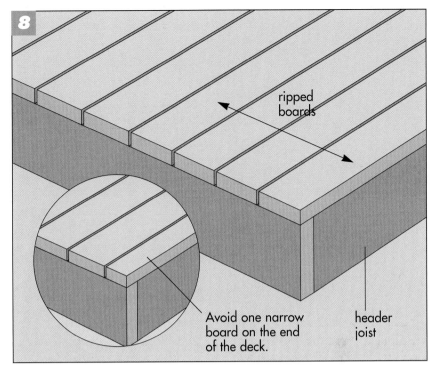

ripped boards

Avoid one narrow board on the end of the deck.

header joist

8. Plan ahead.

When you get down to the last three or four rows of decking, start planning ahead for the last row. Chances are that full-width boards won't fit perfectly, and you should avoid installing one narrow board at the end. Instead, rip small amounts off the last several rows of boards, while maintaining the same gap between boards. Let the end row overhang the header joist by the same amount as the overhang on the sides.

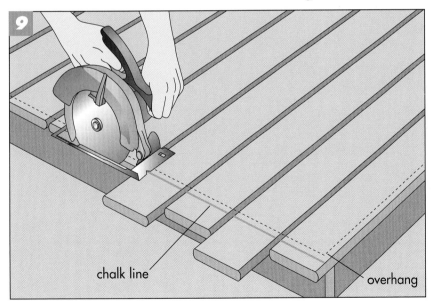

chalk line

overhang

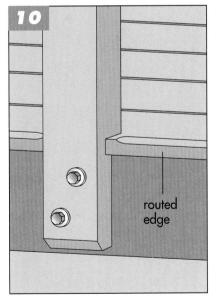

routed edge

9. Trim the edges.

When you've installed all the decking, snap a chalk line along the edges to mark the intended cutoff line. Check that the overhang is the same on all three sides. Set the blade of the circular saw so it just clears the bottom of the decking. Carefully cut the decking by following the chalk line. If you are concerned about cutting a straight line, tack a long, straight board on the decking as a saw guide.

10. Round the edges.

To prevent the wood from splintering and to enhance the beauty of your deck, round the sharp edges of the decking. Use a router equipped with a round-over bit (see page 27).

INSTALLING RAILINGS

Railings are intended to prevent falls, but this basic function doesn't preclude the desire for a creative design. To the deck user, the decking surface may seem the most important and visible part of a deck. To neighbors and passersby, however, the railing is the most obvious feature. Legal code requirements dictate what constitutes a safe deck (see right). Beyond that there are an endless number of design choices and construction techniques.

The most common railings are similar to the traditional picket fence. A typical framework consists of 4×4 posts spanned by a 2×4 or 2×6 cap rail and a 2×4 bottom rail. Balusters attached to these rails provide the style.

The illustrations on these two pages show one simple, attractive design. Another option is a completely enclosed railing. Faced with siding and open only at the bottom for drainage, it provides more privacy and blocks wind.

To prevent sagging railings, keep the spans between posts less than 6 feet. The posts should be bolted to the frame of the deck; use two $\frac{7}{16}$-inch bolts for each connection. Notched posts are the best-looking choice. Cut a notch 1½ inches deep on the bottom of the post and about 8 inches long. Using this technique, you can use shorter bolts and the posts won't protrude so much from the side of the deck. If your decking overhangs the edge of the deck, cut an opening for the post.

YOU'LL NEED

TIME: 1 to 2 days, depending on the size and complexity of the railing.
SKILLS: Basic carpentry skills.
TOOLS: Circular saw, chisel, tape measure, pencil, hammer, power miter saw (optional).

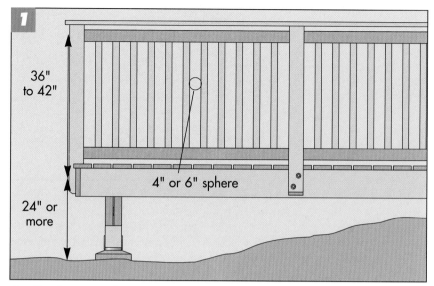

1. Check your code.

When a deck is 24 inches or more above ground, most building codes require a railing. Usually the railing must be between 36 and 42 inches high and must have balusters spaced close enough to prevent a 4- or 6-inch-diameter sphere from passing through them. (The sphere is intended to represent a child's head.) Before you begin railing construction check with your local building department to review codes.

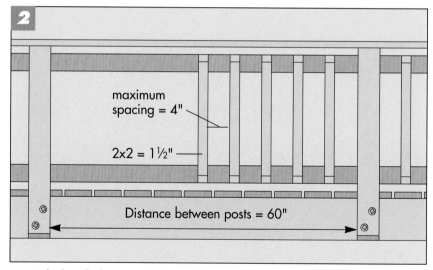

2. Calculate baluster spacing.

Local building codes define the maximum gap between balusters. Getting evenly spaced balusters requires some math (numbers here refer to the above drawing). Add the width of a baluster to that of the maximum spacing and divide this figure into the total distance between posts [(60÷(1.5+4)=10.9]. Round up the result to find the number of required balusters (11).

Then to find the actual spacing between balusters, multiply the number of balusters by the width of one (11×1.5=16.5). Subtract that result from the total distance between posts (60-16.5=43.5). Divide the remainder by the number of spacings (always one more than the number of balusters) to determine the final spacing between balusters (43.5÷12=3.625 or 3⅝ inches).

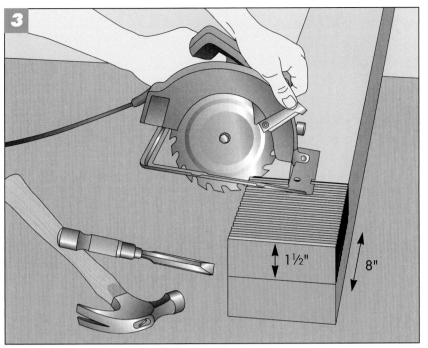

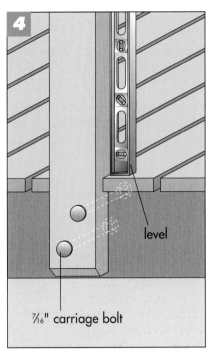

3. Notch railing posts.

Measure a distance equal to the joist depth, less ½ inch, and mark the inside face. Use a circular saw or a tablesaw to make a series of closely spaced cuts 1½ inches deep up to the line. Knock out the pieces with a hammer, then use a chisel to clean out the notch. Cut a 45-degree bevel on the bottom outside corner. If decking will overhang the deck, notch the decking for the post, leaving an ⅛-inch gap on each side of the post.

4. Install posts.

Set the post on top of the decking, flush against the joist. Use a level to keep it plumb and drill two holes through the post and joist. Secure each post with 5-inch-long, ⁷⁄₁₆-inch carriage bolts, using washers on both sides.

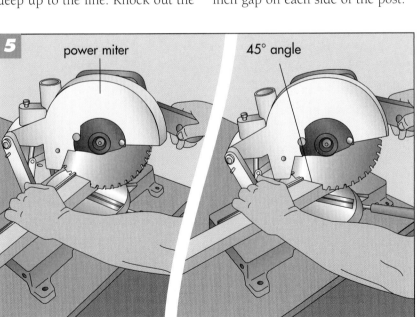

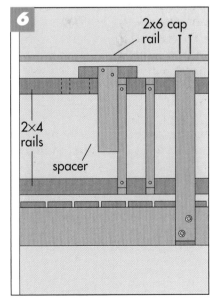

5. Cut balusters.

Cut the balusters from 2×2 stock. Clamp four to six pieces together and cut them all at once with a circular saw. For a large number of repetitive cuts you may want to rent or buy a power miter saw. When cutting pieces with square and beveled ends, cut each baluster roughly to size with square ends. Then add a stop block (a simple jig fastened to the saw base) at the intended baluster length. Finish the baluster with the 45-degree bevel cut.

6. Install rails and balusters.

Install 2×4 top and bottom rails equally spaced from the top of the post and the deck surface. Attach a 2×6 cap rail to the posts. Measure and mark a layout for the balusters or make a spacer as shown. Attach balusters with 8d nails.

BUILDING STAIRS

Unless your deck is within a step of the ground, you will need to build stairs. Building codes usually are quite strict about stair dimensions, although exterior stairs are often afforded more latitude than interior stairs.

Stair building lingo can be confusing at first. Rise is the vertical distance from one tread to the next; run is the horizontal depth of the tread. The total rise and total run are the overall vertical and horizontal measurements of the stairs.

For greatest stepping comfort, try to build deck stairs with a 6- to 7-inch rise and an 11- to 16-inch run. The large range in run distances is because you can use either two or three 2×6s for each tread. The deeper treads can be a safety feature when stairs are wet or covered with snow and ice.

Stairs that are 3 feet wide are comfortable and safe, and may be mandated by your local code. Use three stringers on 3-foot-wide stairs. Although you can get by with two stringers on narrower stairs, the time and cost of making that extra stringer are minimal. If you build wider stairs, add an additional stringer for every 2 feet of stair width.

YOU'LL NEED

TIME: After the concrete pad is completed, 1 hour to lay out and cut each stringer and 3 hours to attach stringers to deck and attach treads.
SKILLS: Working with concrete (if a pad is added), measuring and laying out, leveling, accurate cutting and fastening.
TOOLS: Hammer, straightedge, tape measure, pencil, level, framing square, circular saw, handsaw.

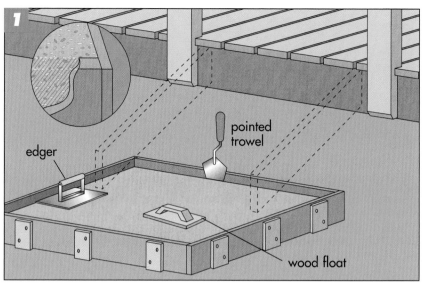

1. Prepare the concrete pad.
Excavate and build forms for a 4-inch concrete pad set on 6 inches of gravel. Mix and pour concrete. Screed the surface with a 2×4, then smooth it with a wood float. Run a pointed trowel between the concrete and form boards; follow with an edger. After an hour, smooth the concrete with a steel trowel. Or, prepare a bed of tamped gravel at least 6 inches deep. See page 58 for how to attach stringers to the footings.

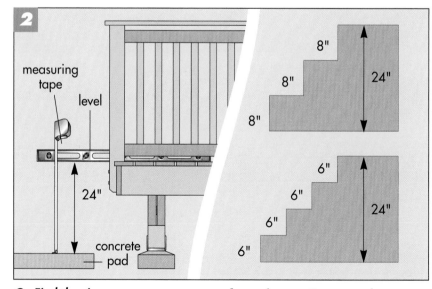

2. Find the rise.
Use a level to extend the deck to the spot where the stairs will land (usually the pad or gravel bed). Measure the total rise and divide by 7 (the height of an ideal rise). The result, rounded to the nearest whole number, is the ideal number of risers for the stairs. Now divide the total rise by the number of risers to determine the actual rise for each step. For example, assume the total rise is 24 inches; 24 divided by 7 is 3.4. Round 3.4 down to 3 and divide this into 24. The result (8 inches) is the rise for each step. An 8-inch rise is on the high side so you can take the option of rounding 3.4 up to 4, then dividing 4 into 24, for a more comfortable rise of 6 inches (with 4 risers rather than 3).

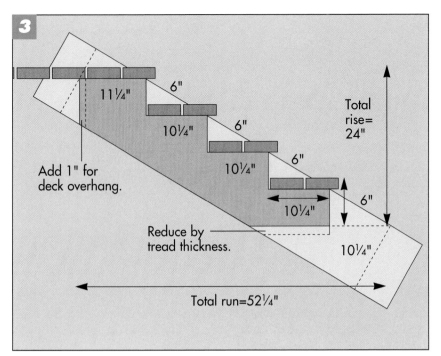

3. *Find the run.*
If you're not constrained by space, choose a convenient, comfortable tread depth: Two 2×6s for each tread, with gaps between them for drainage, and a 1-inch overhang.

The resulting run is 10¼ inches. Estimate the length of a 2×10 or 2×12 stringer you'll need by measuring from where the stringer connects with deck to the ground-level riser.

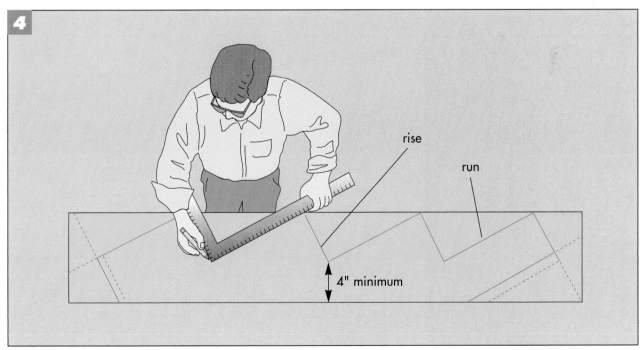

4. *Make the stringers.*
For 3-foot-wide stairs cut three identical stringers. Lay out and cut the first one, then use it as a template to lay out the other two.

To lay out the stringer, place a framing square on a stringer so the 6-inch mark on the outside of the square's tongue and the 10⅛-inch mark on the outside of the square's blade both align with the top edge of the stringer. Mark the rise and run along the outside of the square. Move the square and repeat. Mark an additional cutoff of 1½ inches off the bottom and add the amount of the decking overhang at the top.

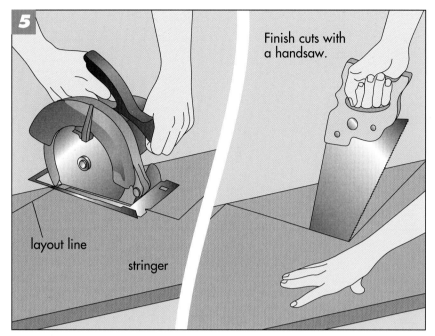

Finish cuts with a handsaw.

layout line

stringer

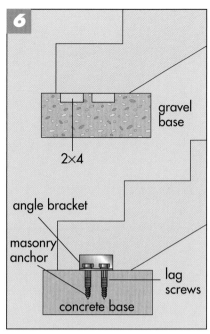

gravel base

2×4

angle bracket

masonry anchor

lag screws

concrete base

5. Cut the stringers.

With the layout completely marked on the first stringer, carefully cut it out with a circular saw. Cut only up to the layout marks. Where the tread and riser meet, the circular saw blade won't cut all the way through. Finish the cuts with a handsaw. Set the stringer in place and check the accuracy of your layout. Once you're assured all the markings are correct, use the cut stringer as a template for cutting the others.

6. Attach stringers to footing.

On a gravel pad, attach two 36-inch 2×4s to the bottoms of the stringers and embed the 2×4s in the gravel. On a concrete pad, space outside stringers 36 inches apart, center the middle stringer, and attach with masonry anchors.

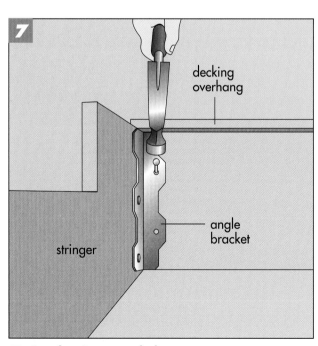

decking overhang

angle bracket

stringer

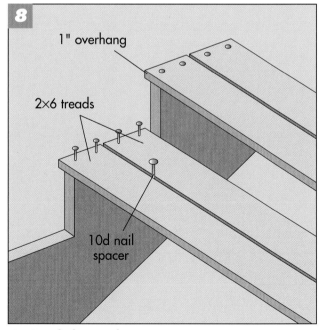

1" overhang

2×6 treads

10d nail spacer

7. Attach stringers to deck.

Stringers must be installed straight and square. The top should be level with the top of the joist, slipping directly under the overhanging deck boards. Use angle brackets or framing anchors to attach stringers to the joist. As with any structural bracket, use only the fasteners recommended by the manufacturer.

8. Attach the treads.

Each tread is made of two pieces of 2×6 decking. Cut each 38 inches long to provide a 1-inch overhang on each of the outer stringers. Use a 10d nail to measure the gap between treads and between the back tread and the stringer. The treads should overhang the front of the stringers by 1 inch as well.

9

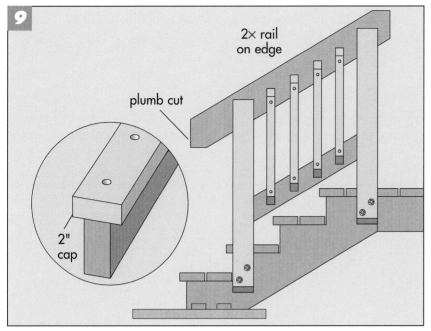

2× rail on edge

plumb cut

2" cap

9. Build the railing.

The stair railing should match the style of your deck's railing as much as possible. Use similar balusters, spaced the same distance apart. One important difference, however, is the handrail must be grasped easily. This can be accomplished by setting a 2× top rail on edge so it can be grasped. Even better, place a 2-inch-wide cap on the top rail for optimum safety. Prepare and fasten posts and balusters as you did for the deck railing. Make plumb cuts on the top rail.

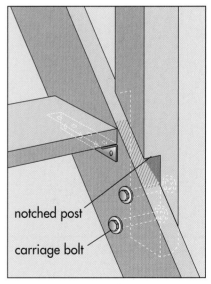

CAUTION!
FOR COMFORT AND SAFETY, ADD HANDRAILS

Municipal building codes generally require a railing on stairs with three or more risers. But there is almost no stair that can't be made safer by adding a railing. Having a solid object to grasp when stepping from one plane to the next is a bit of comfort that most of us can appreciate. Take the trouble to add this safety feature, especially if your deck is going to be used by a child or an elderly person. Think safety even if your deck has a one-step level change. Avoid stumbles by adding a strip of yellow reflective tape to assure the step up or down will be seen by the user.

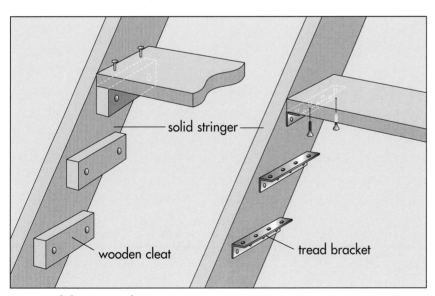

solid stringer

wooden cleat

tread bracket

Use a solid stringer alternative.

The strongest stairs are made with treads sitting on top of notched stringers. But some people don't care for the appearance, preferring to mask the tread ends with solid stringers. You still need to lay out stringers, but instead of cutting them, you install tread brackets or wooden cleats to the inside of the stringers. Once the stringers are attached to the deck, treads are cut to fit between the stringers and are fastened to the brackets or cleats. If you use this method on a wide stair, you should still prepare a notched middle stringer.

notched post

carriage bolt

Notch posts on solid stringers.

Posts on solid-stringer stairs must be prepared differently as well. Notch the post if you like. Set it in place, checking for plumb, then mark an angled line where it touches the stringer (top and bottom). Cut the notch and fasten it with carriage bolts.

Using Complex Decking Patterns

Usually, the simplest decking pattern is the easiest and most cost-efficient. For most decks, that means installing deck boards parallel with the house. But if you'd prefer something more interesting, the illustration at *right* shows some decking patterns from which you can choose.

Many of these patterns have special framing requirements to support the decking adequately and allow drainage where the decking pieces meet. That means foundations and framing plans must be adjusted. Always plan for a double joist for joints between decking boards. This ensures a solid nailing surface for decking boards and encourages water drainage through the deck.

On a narrow deck, you often can cover the span with a single board, and you won't need the double joist. However, on a wide deck you'll need a double joist where the decking pattern repeats and a new section of decking begins. Note that with some patterns, for example, the diamond pattern, boards are a variety of lengths. Be aware that these kinds of patterns create extra work and extra waste.

CAUTION!
Check Diagonals for Allowable Spans
If you use a diagonal or herringbone pattern, use the distance along the decking between joists to calculate the allowable span, not the perpendicular distance between joists. If you have doubts about the suitability of your design, have a professional deck designer or architect check it before you begin construction.

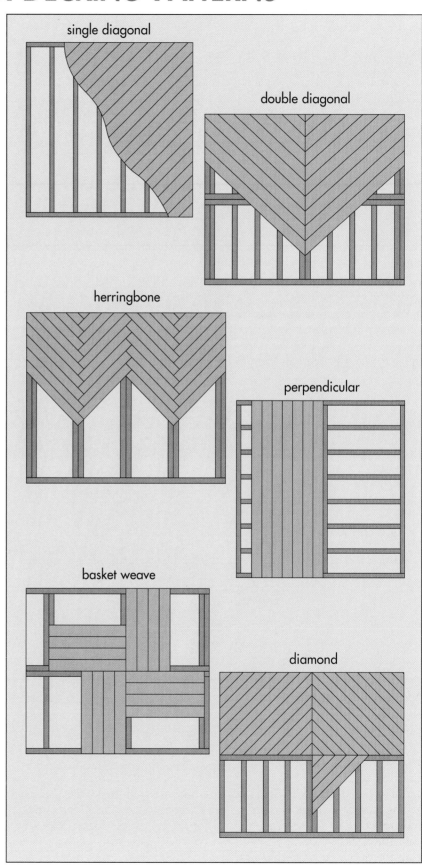

single diagonal

double diagonal

herringbone

perpendicular

basket weave

diamond

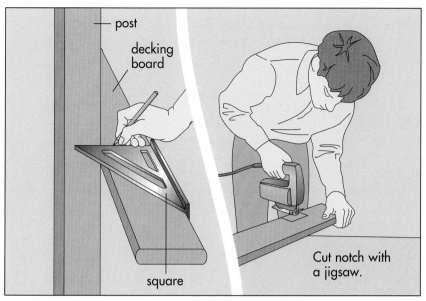

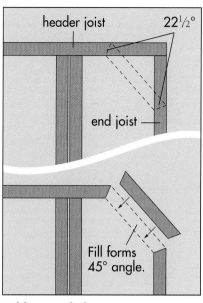

Notch decking around posts.

To notch decking to fit around a post or other obstruction, lay the board as closely as possible to where it will be placed and square it with the obstruction. Use a square to transfer the post width onto the board. Measure and mark the depth of the cut. To provide a gap for drainage, add about 1/8 inch on each side of the cut. Carefully cut along these marks with a sabersaw. Test the fit and trim as needed.

Add an angled corner.

If the style suits your house, add a 45-degree corner where the joists overhang the beam. Build the corner square, then measure an equal distance from the corner on each joist. Cut joists at a 22 1/2-degree angle, then mark and cut a piece to fill in the angle.

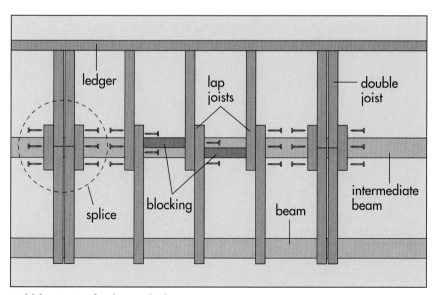

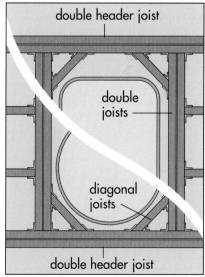

Add lap joists for large decks.

Building a large deck involves little more than duplicating the procedures for building a basic deck. For example, if you want a wider deck, plan to add extra double joists to provide staggered nailing surfaces for the ends of decking boards. Likewise, if you want the deck to extend farther from the house, add another line of foundation posts to handle an extra beam. Note that for this kind of extension, joists must be lapped over an intermediate beam. Drive in 16d nails on both sides of the lap joist to make a solid connection. Blocking may be required to provide added support for the lap joists. Toenail blocking into lap joists with 16d nails.

Frame around a hot tub or tree.

To build an opening in the deck for a hot tub or tree, add double header joists, then double the joists on either side. Finish framing around the opening with short diagonal joists. For a hot tub, cover with decking, then cut the hole. For a tree, trim decking a couple of inches short of touching the trunk to allow for growth.

INSTALLING OPTIONAL RAILING DESIGNS

Deciding what kind of railing to put on your deck is one of the most important design decisions you'll make. Railings are the most visible part of the deck when viewed from the yard or the street, so they'll have a big impact on the look of the deck. Because some railing styles require posts that run continuously up from the footing, you need to plan your railing before you set the posts.

Think about the material you use to build the railing. Just because you build the rest of the deck with pressure-treated pine doesn't mean the railing has to be the same. Given the high visibility of the railing, you may want to use a more attractive alternative, such as cedar or redwood.

On the other hand, you may want to paint the railing to match or complement your house. In this case, pressure-treated pine would be a logical and less-expensive choice even if you use cedar or redwood for the decking.

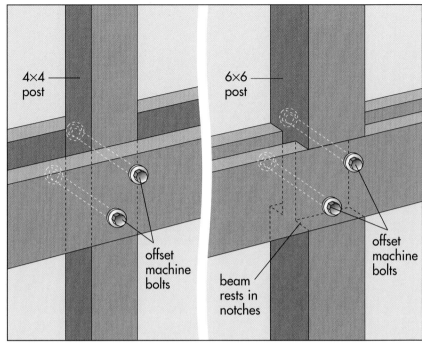

Choose an optional post design.
Deck posts can serve double duty by supporting a beam and continuing up to carry a railing, bench, or overhead structure. With a 4×4 continuous post, the beam should be composed of 2×s attached to each side with carriage or machine bolts. This connection is not as sturdy as when the beam rests on top of the posts. Another option is to use a 6×6 post, resting the beams in notches. This requires a little more preparation and labor, but adds strength and stability to the deck.

Select a post connection.
Posts bolted to the end or header joists can be strengthened with blocking. This is especially recommended on high decks or if the post will be subjected to heavier-than-normal loads. Blocking must be added from below or before the decking is installed. For header joists, cut a piece of joist stock to fit between the joists and nail it behind the post, as shown at *near right*. Bolt through the post, joist, and blocking. For end joists, insert blocking behind the post on one or both sides, as shown at *far right*.

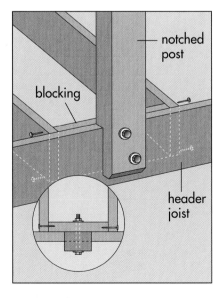

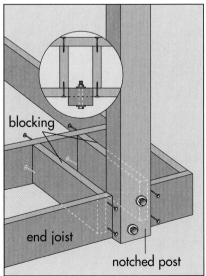

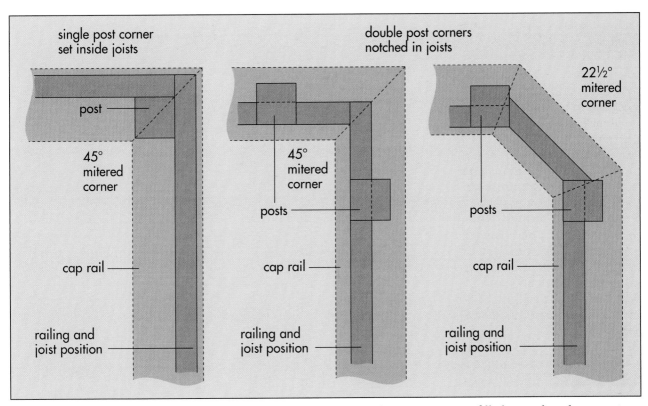

Turn railing corners.

Here are three techniques you can use for handling the railing at corners. These can be adapted to suit many different railing designs. In each of these options the railing is positioned directly above the end joists. If you want to use a single post in the corner, place it and other rail posts inside the joists. Or you can use two posts set back equidistant from the corner. They can be placed close enough together to meet code requirements, or they can be set apart a bit, as shown, with the space filled in with a short section of the railing. The double posts provide a solid surface for the cap rail, which can support either a 45-degree miter or a 22½-degree mitered section.

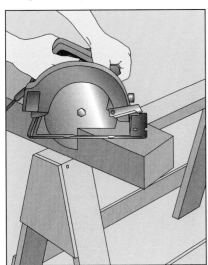

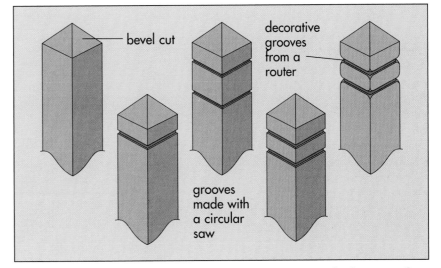

Decorate the posts.

Don't settle for a flat post top. Take a few minutes to decorate the post using a circular saw or tablesaw. Cut identical bevels on each side of the post to create a pointed cap. Not only is this more attractive, it also sheds water and adds longevity to the post. You also can cut grooves around the posts. Sketch out the design you want, then mark cut lines on each post. Using a circular saw or tablesaw, make a single pass for a thin groove or multiple passes for a wider groove. Or use a router with any one of several router bits to make decorative grooves. Getting grooves to line up around the post is tricky. Practice first on some scrap material.

Use post brackets.

The folks who make joist hangers, post anchors, seismic ties, and other metal gadgets for joining wood to wood also make a variety of useful brackets for constructing a railing. Several types of brackets are available for securing rail posts to joists. These same brackets also can be used for posts on the stairs. Using brackets saves time, and in some cases they may be your only option for attaching posts.

However, posts attached with brackets won't be as secure as posts bolted to the frame, and the brackets may detract from the appearance of your deck. Brackets also can be useful for attaching rails to posts. The type shown at *lower right* secures a cap rail while remaining out of sight.

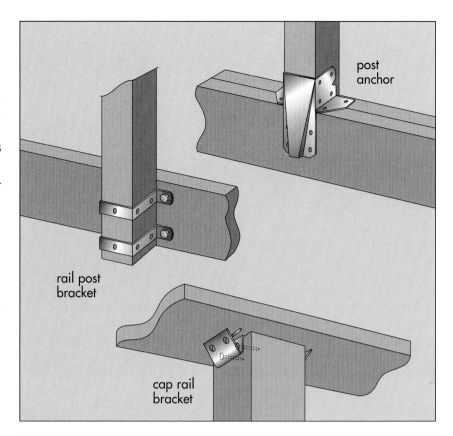

Choose ready-made components.

Traditionally-styled homes shouldn't have decks that look like helipads. Meld your deck with your home by using decorative post caps, spindles, and finials.

Home centers and lumberyards carry many styles of decorative railing parts. Turned balusters, also called spindles, have a traditional look that suits older homes. You usually can find posts with a matching design. Post caps and screw-in finials, often used in combination, quickly transform a drab post top to an eye-catching feature of your deck.

Ready-made railing parts can be used separately or bought as a complete package containing all of the pieces you need to put your railing together. Some ready-made railings are manufactured from plastic. You won't find one that looks like wood, but if you intend to paint the railing anyway, it might pay to consider this option. Just be sure to choose railing parts that are suitable for outdoor use.

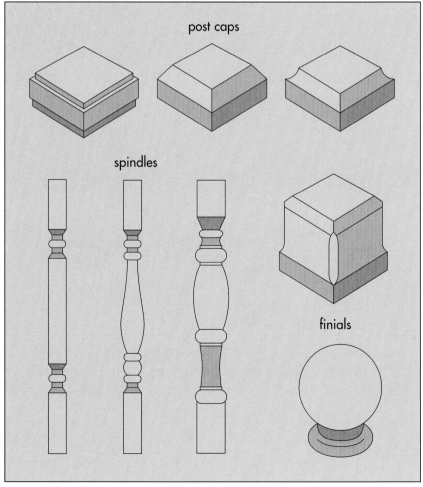

Choose rail and baluster styles.

As long as you meet code requirements for spacing and height, what you use to fill in the spaces between posts is largely up to you. Rails installed "on edge" and attached to the inside or outside face of the posts are least likely to sag. Rails also can be positioned on their flat sides, "on flat," and set between posts, resting on rail brackets or cleats or set into dadoes cut in the posts. Balusters for either system can be identical. The difference is they are nailed on the side of the on-edge rails or at the top and bottom of the on-flat rails.

Railings can be filled in with a variety of materials. Copper or galvanized steel tubing can be used in place of wood balusters. Copper can be coated to preserve its existing color or allowed to age to a graceful blue-green. Steel can be used as it is or painted. Clear acrylic sheets are ideal for maintaining an open view. Some homeowners welded hog fencing to make a surprisingly strong and good-looking railing infill.

Balusters do not have to be vertical. A simple railing can be made with 1×4s or 2×4s attached horizontally to the posts. Metal tubing or wood dowels are attractive when used in this way. Keep in mind, however, that in the eyes of most children, horizontal balusters make an ideal ladder. A railing that encourages climbing can be dangerous, especially if there is a chance of falling over the side. Also, the extra weight and abuse the balusters must bear require they be strong and fastened solidly.

Lattice infill provides more privacy than standard railings, yet allows plenty of air to circulate. The lattice can be fixed in place with stops nailed to the posts and to the top and bottom flat rails (see page 74).

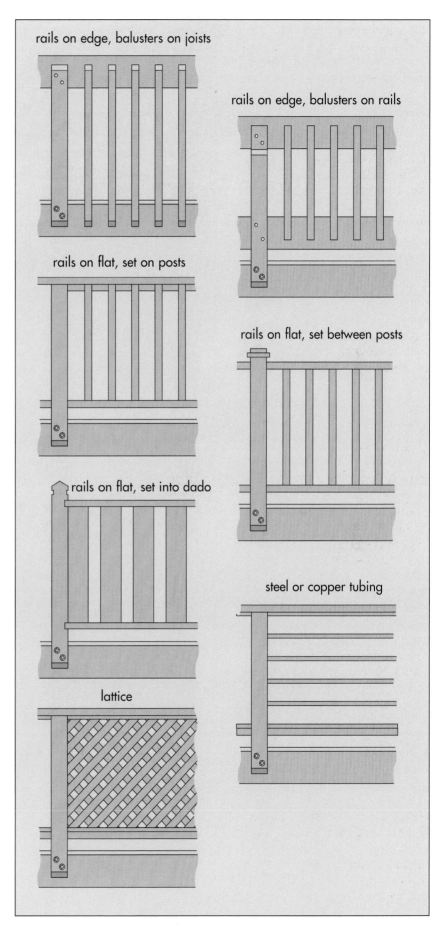

rails on edge, balusters on joists

rails on edge, balusters on rails

rails on flat, set on posts

rails on flat, set between posts

rails on flat, set into dado

steel or copper tubing

lattice

BUILDING PLANTERS

Planters overflowing with annuals and perennials can soften the lines of your deck, helping to blend it to your yard.

Make planters 18 to 24 inches deep if you're planning to plant shrubs or bushes. Planters for annuals can be smaller. Line planters with waterproof material for longer planter life and provide drainage in the bottom of the planter by using slats or plywood with holes bored in it. Always build planters with 1 to 2 inches of space beneath them to allow for air circulation.

YOU'LL NEED

TIME: 1 to 2 hours, depending on the planter.
SKILLS: Cutting, fastening.
TOOLS: Circular saw, hammer or cordless screwdriver, speed square, framing square.

RECYCLE DECK SCRAPS

When you've paid top dollar for good quality lumber, the last thing you want to do is send it to the landfill or burn it as kindling. (Warning: Never burn pressure-treated lumber. Burning will release toxins into the air.) Instead, save scraps for small outdoor projects.

After building a deck, you'll likely have enough scrap to build a planter or two. Locate the planters in corners or along the edges of the deck. Pressure-treated wood is fine for planters, but use only rot-resistant, non-treated wood, such as redwood or cedar, for other outdoor items, for example, small lawn tables, bird-houses, or a sandbox.

Ornament with planters.
Decks by their nature are intended to tie the indoors to the outdoors. Plants help reinforce that theme on any deck. Decks low enough that they don't need a railing are particularly easy to build, but they can be a bit boring. Many low decks look as though they aren't finished yet; they seem to call out for more attention. A border of flowers adds color, of course, but it also helps define and complete the structure.

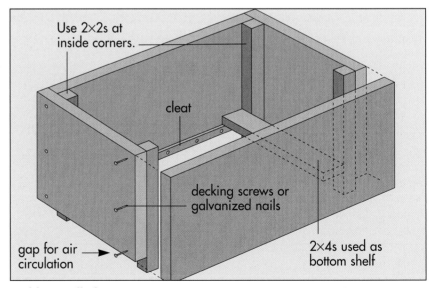

Build a small planter.
Build this planter from 2×8 or 2×10 pieces. Simply cut them to size and fasten the inside-corner 2×2s to the end pieces with 2½-inch decking screws or 12d nails. Regardless of the style of planter, build it with feet or legs that allow air to circulate beneath it. Move the planter from time to time so moisture and mildew will not build up underneath it. Fasten cleats to the insides of the planters to hold a bottom shelf, which can actually be set at any height. Drill holes to provide drainage or use spaced 2×4s instead.

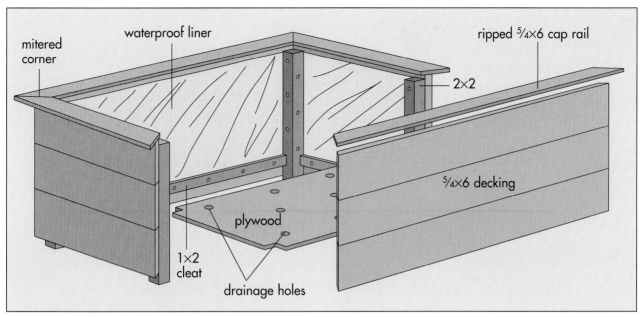

waterproof liner

mitered corner

ripped ⁵⁄₄×6 cap rail

2×2

⁵⁄₄×6 decking

plywood

1×2 cleat

drainage holes

Use decking planter for annuals or small perennials.

Use leftover ⁵⁄₄×6 decking for the sides of this planter. Cut four 24-inch pieces for inside the corners from scrap 2×2 baluster stock. Cut the decking to the lengths you want. Miter the corner joints for a professional look. Apply plastic sheeting or roofing felt on the decking material before attaching the 2×2s with leftover deck screws or 8d galvanized finishing nails. Allow the 2×2s to extend an inch or so below the bottom of the planter for air circulation. Drill drainage holes in the ½- or ¾-inch plywood floor of the planter. Attach the floor to the cleats with 1-inch deck screws. Finally, a mitered cap rail of ripped ⁵⁄₄×6 decking finishes off the planter.

Make a large planter.

Most deck-building projects leave a small pile of 4×4 scraps lying around. Here's a good way to put them to use. Use the scraps to provide vertical support for a planter, while doubling as a nailing surface for the side pieces. This technique is particularly useful for large planters; the finished size is limited only by the size of boards and posts in your scrap heap. Cut four 4×4s to the same length. Attach 2× scraps to the sides with 3-inch deck screws or 16d galvanized nails, lapping each board at the corner. Set the bottom boards about an inch above the bottom of the posts. Finish with a cap rail, mitered at each corner. Place this planter over a potted plant. Or enclose the bottom with plywood or board slats and add soil for shrubs and annuals. With the added weight of soil this planter may be too heavy to move so set it in place first, then fill it.

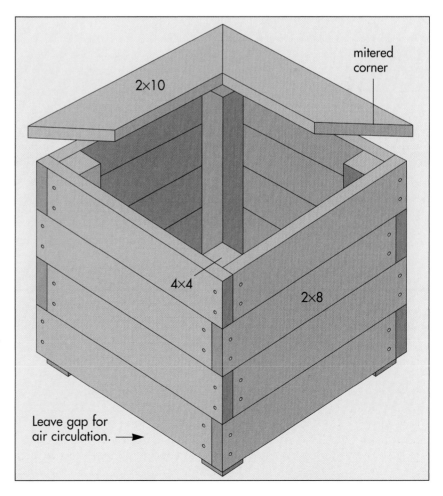

2×10

mitered corner

4×4

2×8

Leave gap for air circulation. →

CONSTRUCTING DECK SEATING

Benches can be part of the perimeter or define separate areas of a deck. Best of all, they give a deck a welcome livability. Benches should be between 15 and 18 inches high with seats at least 15 inches deep. For comfortable lounging, you might want seats up to 30 inches deep. Here are plans for a built-in bench and a movable bench. They can serve as starting points for creating benches that suit your deck style. Adjust height, depth, and length to meet your needs. (For attaching benches to a railing, see page 70.)

YOU'LL NEED

TIME: Several hours for the freestanding bench; up to a full weekend for built-ins.
SKILLS: Basic carpentry and deck-building skills.
TOOLS: Circular saw, drill, socket wrench, screwdriver, hammer, sander, router.

CAUTION

DON'T SUBSTITUTE SEATING FOR RAILING

Built-in perimeter seating should not be viewed as a substitute for a railing. If you build a 15-inch-high bench on a deck requiring a 36-inch-high railing, building inspectors likely will insist that the railing behind the bench be 51 inches high.
This is because people, especially children, will stand on the benches. The railing needs to be built higher to afford the same protection against a fall as it does on the deck surface.

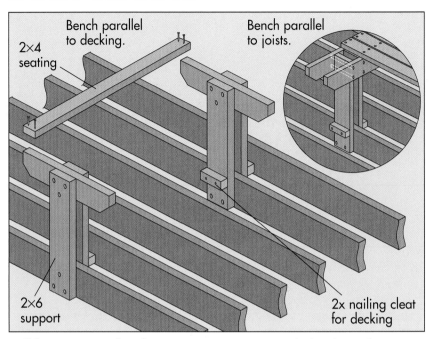

Build a permanent bench.
Benches or short tables can be built into about any part of a deck using the above technique. Attach the legs before you install the decking, or temporarily remove decking. To attach the supports, use carriage bolts above the decking and machine bolts below it. Add supports for every 4 feet of bench length. Use 2×4s or 2×2s for the seat itself. This design can be used no matter which way the joists and decking run.

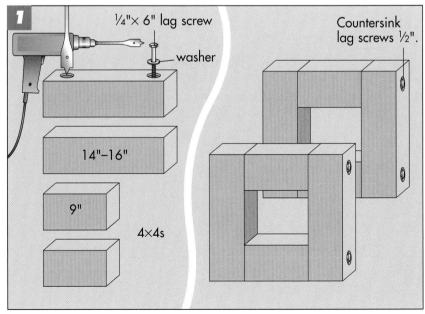

1. Build a movable bench.
Begin by assembling base units out of four pieces of 4×4 post scraps cut to the dimensions shown or to those that suit your needs. Use a tablesaw or power miter saw to cut the 4×4s square. Set the pieces on a flat surface and drill pilot holes. Counterbore holes for the lag screws and washers. Fasten the parts together. Make one base for every 3 feet of bench length.

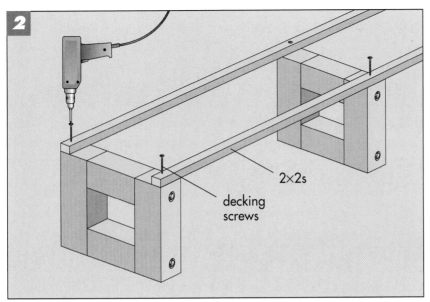

2. Attach seat boards.

Lay out 2×2 or 2×4 seat pieces, choosing a gap of between ⅛ and ½ inch. Our design, using nine 2×2s, has an ⅛-inch gap between the boards. Work on a flat surface and make sure the 2×2s are as straight as possible. Start by attaching the end seat boards with decking screws. Before attaching the rest of the 2×2s, lay them in place to make sure they fit with an equal gap between them.

EXPERTS' INSIGHT

BUY READY-MADE DECK SEATING

If you don't need a custom-built table or bench or one that's bolted down, you can buy pre-built furniture that matches the style of your deck.

Adirondack chairs, for example, often are available in the same wood species typically used in deck construction. Look for unfinished chairs and a matching table, and finish them with the same sealer or stain you use on the deck. A picnic table with benches is another natural choice for furnishing a deck.

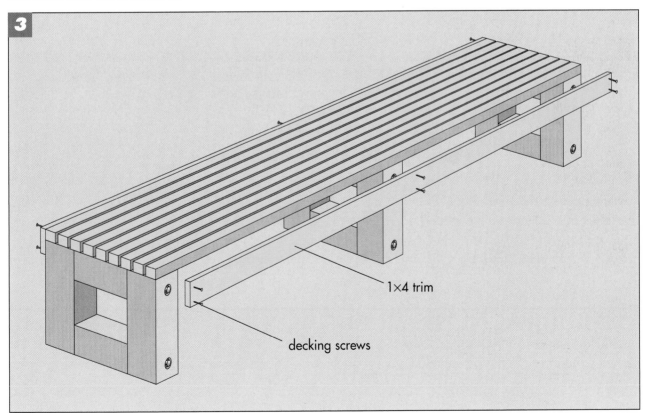

3. Finish the bench.

Drive the screw heads ⅛ inch below the surface. Cut two 1×4 trim boards and attach them with decking screws driven into the seat and the bases. Sand the seat carefully. Then relieve the sharp edges with sandpaper or a router equipped with a round-over bit (see page 27). Apply finish to match the deck. This bench can be moved as needed and can rest on a flat surface in the yard.

ATTACHING SEATING TO RAILINGS

Built-in deck seating must be designed to carry a heavy load. The framing for the seating should be tied into a part of the deck designed to handle such weight. A perimeter bench is easy to build, and because it is supported by the railing posts it doesn't require much extra lumber.

Posts should be located no more than 3 feet apart to provide satisfactory support. Seating like this can line the entire perimeter of the deck, run along one side, or be placed in a corner. Use the same type of wood on the bench as on the decking and railing.

YOU'LL NEED

TIME: Up to a full day to construct one section.
SKILLS: Measuring, cutting, fastening.
TOOLS: Circular saw, drill, hammer, sanding block or power sander.

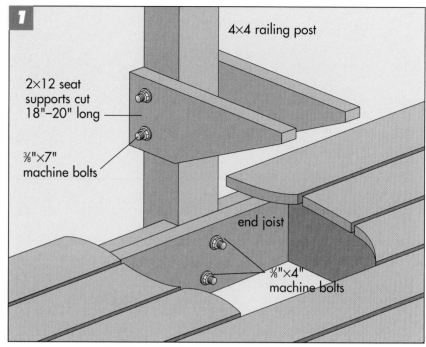

1. Attach bench supports.
Bench supports should be bolted to the 4×4 railing posts. If posts are spaced more than 3 feet apart, bolt intermediate posts to the joist. The posts must be bolted securely to the deck framing, and blocking should be installed (see page 62). Use ⅜×7-inch machine bolts to attach a pair of 2×12 seat supports to each post. Cut supports 18 to 20 inches long and taper them for clearance beneath the bench.

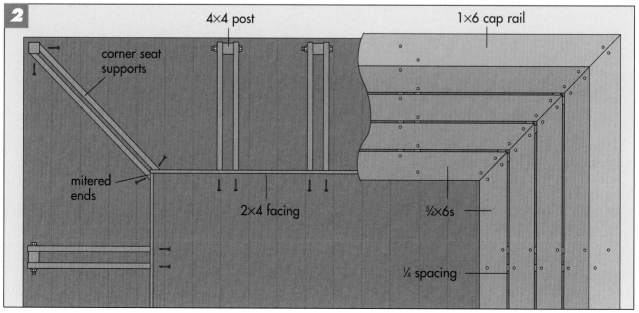

2. Attach seat boards.
Attach ⁵⁄₄×6 decking across the top of the seat supports for the bench seat. Space them ¼ inch apart and secure them with 2½-inch decking screws. Trim the front edge with a 2×4 attached to the ends of the supports. If you install a bench in a corner, the corner seat supports will have to be longer. Install the 2×4 facing, mitering the ends. Then measure, cut, and install the corner supports. Sand the rough edges or round over the front edge with a router.

BUILDING OVERHEAD STRUCTURES

Overhead structures can provide function and beauty for your deck. In addition to blocking the sun's rays, the strategically placed slats or boards are attractive architectural features. Even minimal overhead structures give a deck a higher profile, enhancing the deck's role as transition between indoors and outdoors. They also are useful for defining areas of the deck.

Overhead structures can provide complete or minimal shading. Often they shade an eating area, add privacy to a hot tub, or double as a trellis. Overhead structures are easiest to build when designed along with the original deck because all of the structural details can be incorporated into the deck construction. Adding an overhead to an existing deck can be more difficult; posts must be attached to joists. Ideally, overhead posts should rest on footings.

DON'T OVERLOAD

Deck overheads don't have to be built to accommodate the weight of people and furniture. Therefore, they can be made of relatively lightweight materials. A simple overhead composed of well-spaced, uncovered slats or boards does not stress the structure of your deck as long as the posts are sized adequately and supported firmly. However, a solid roof or other structure that will add substantial weight to the deck framing infrastructure should be designed by a professional. In cold climates an overhead may have to support a heavy snow load, even if the overhead itself is lightweight.

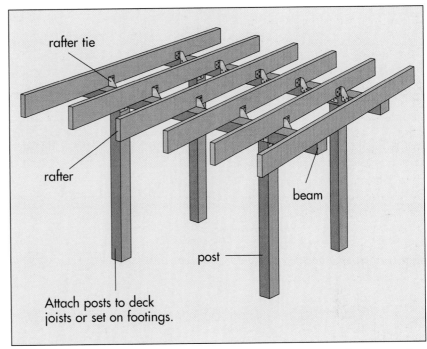

Build a freestanding overhead.
An overhead on a freestanding deck, or one intended to cover only part of a large deck, can be supported by beams spanning the posts. In either case, the overhead must rest on posts, which must be connected either directly to the footings or secured to the deck framing. You may want to consider installing new posts and new footings to support the overhead.

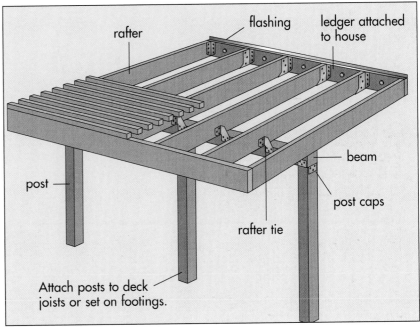

Attach an overhead to the house.
Overheads can be supported in part by a second ledger attached to the house (see pages 36–37 for ledger installation). Add a beam supported by posts fastened to the deck joists or set on post footings. Attach the beam with brackets, using fasteners recommended by the manufacturer.

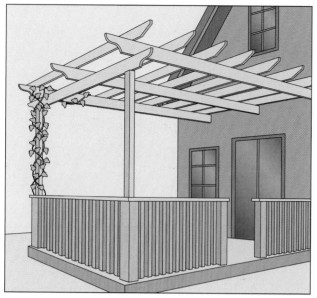

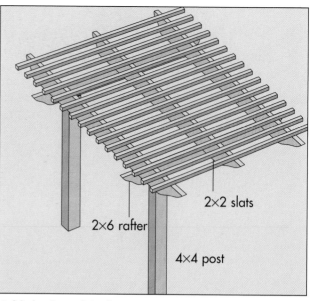

Create an outdoor room.

This overhead adds a moderate amount of shade, but mostly lends the stylish illusion of the deck being an outdoor room, making the deck a true extension of the house. Overheads can double as trellises, another means of tying the deck to the yard.

Add shade with style.

For overheads that offer substantial shading, the most appealing designs use several layers of wood, with each layer composed of smaller pieces spaced closer together. The crisscrossed framing adds stability to the structure and gives the deck more of a profile, yet allows plenty of ventilation and drainage.

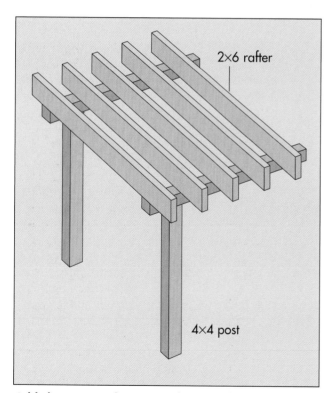

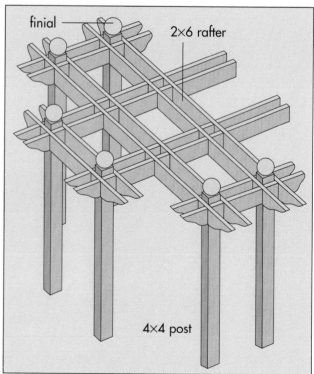

Add character with a minimal approach.

A few boards, spaced carefully, can cut much of the glare from even noonday sun. In addition, the sense of having something overhead can be an important characteristic of a deck.

Make an overhead a prime attraction.

Some overhead structures are designed just for their visual appeal. If style is your primary interest, pay close attention to the details. Try to integrate the design with elements from the rest of the deck or from the house itself. Keep the scale of the overhead in line with its immediate environment.

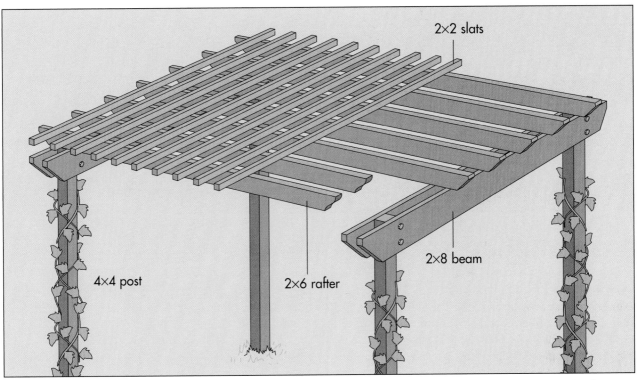

2×2 slats

2×8 beam

4×4 post

2×6 rafter

Vary this basic design to suit your deck.

This overhead is simple to build and can be adapted easily to provide the degree of shading you want. The double 2×8 beams span from post to post or extend from a ledger to posts. The 2×6 rafters set 16 inches on center can safely span beams up to 12 feet apart. Use rafter ties or 10d nails (through both sides) to fasten rafters to beams. Here, the beam and rafter ends have matching tapers. You can use many decorative designs (see *below*). Attach a top layer of 2×2 slats, spaced 4 to 8 inches apart by driving 8d nails through the slats into the rafters. You may be able to use lattice instead of, or on top of, the slats, but check your local building codes first.

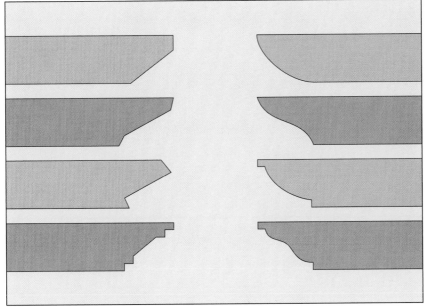

Choose a decorative rafter cut.

A key to designing an attractive overhead structure is to dress up the rafter ends. Find a decorative detail on the house, deck, or in the yard, then transfer that theme to a design for the rafter ends. When you are satisfied with a design, make a template out of plywood, hardboard, or cardboard. Trace the design on each rafter, then make the cut with a sabersaw.

BRACING POSTS

Knowing when to brace posts supporting an overhead structure can be somewhat confusing. Local codes may not offer definitive answers. Generally, if your overhead is lightweight (consisting of loosely spaced slats, for example) and if one side is connected to a ledger at the house, you almost certainly won't need bracing. At the other end of the scale, assume that you should brace the posts for a top-heavy overhead on a freestanding deck. For everything in between, build the overhead without bracing and check the stability of the structure before deciding. For guidance on bracing, see page 99.

FRAMING LATTICE

Lattice is a popular screening material, suitable for overheads and privacy screens. Commonly sold in 4×8-, 2×8-, and 4×6-foot sheets, lattice is decorative and easy to install. Standard panels are ½ inch thick, although you may be able to find a heavier-duty panel made with thicker lath. The size of the spacing also varies. To permanently install lattice, add posts and rails to frame the lattice panels. Add strips of molding between which you can sandwich the panels. Plastic lattice panels look similar to painted wood and are worth considering for their ease of installation and low maintenance requirements.

YOU'LL NEED

TIME: About 1 hour per sheet for standard installation.
SKILLS: Measuring, cutting lattice and trim.
TOOLS: Handsaw or circular saw, hammer, screwdriver or cordless drill, square, tape measure.

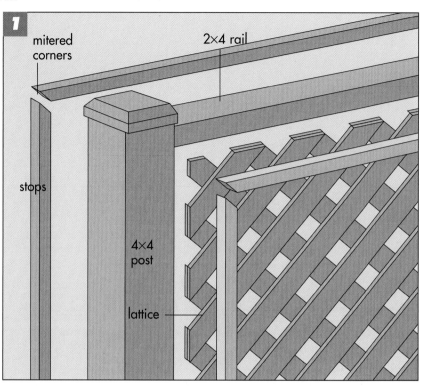

1. Frame the lattice.

Lattice is a convenient means for hiding unsightly views or adding privacy and shading. It also can be added as skirting along the base of the deck. Never use it where it might be stepped on. Lattice normally is bordered by posts and 2× rails. Small wooden strips, called stops, are attached to the posts and rails to sandwich the lattice in place.

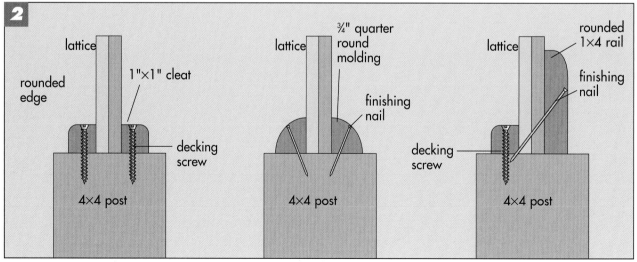

2. Sandwich the panels.

With a well-secured post providing the nailing surface, you can can secure lattice with stops made from a variety of types of trim. Use only pressure-treated or rot-resistant wood and galvanized fasteners. Small square or rectangular stops (1×1 or 2×2) work well, as does ¾-inch quarter round molding. For a bolder look, use 1×4s set on edge for stops and miter the corners. Round the edges with a sander or a router (see page 27). Consider applying a waterproof sealer or stain to all sides of the stops and the edges of the lattice before installation.

BUILDING PRIVACY SCREENS

Decks often need buffering from wind, noise, or an unpleasant view. A railing, a border of planters and benches, or a lattice screen may be sufficient. But for added enclosure, add a screen. When designing or choosing a screen, try to maintain a scale compatible with other elements of the deck. If blocking the wind is your main concern, it's best not to block it entirely with a solid wall. By letting some air circulate through the screen, you'll reduce the load on the framing and get some breeze on hot days.

EXPERTS' INSIGHT

SUPPORT THE SCREEN

The screens on this page are basically adaptations of popular fence styles. Their functions are similar. Both designs can be built as integral parts of the deck's railing. A small screen can be supported by posts bolted to the deck framing. A large screen should be connected to posts resting on the footings. This is especially important if the screen will be subjected to heavy winds. You also may be able to accomplish your objectives by installing a screen or a fence a short distance from the deck.

Weave a screen.
A simple basket weave screen is one of the easiest and least expensive options for a privacy and wind screen. The trick is to use thin boards, ⅜ to ½ inches thick and 4 to 8 inches wide.

(These may have to be special ordered.) Use 1×2 or 2×2 stops on the posts to contain the boards, and 1×2 vertical spacers. Adjust the undulation by varying the size and spacing between the spacers.

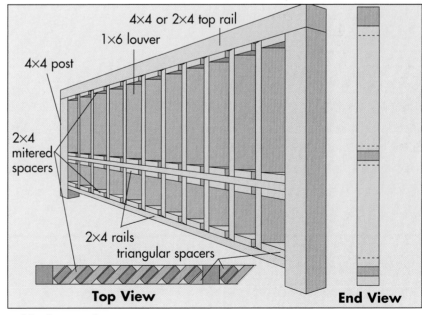

Add a louvered screen.
This louvered screen is complex to build, but provides added privacy while allowing cooling breezes to flow through. The angle, spacing, and direction of the louvers can be adjusted for the desired effect. The louvers are 1×6s, spaced by mitered spacers cut from a 2×4. These repetitive cuts are best done with a power miter saw or tablesaw. The 4×4 top rail adds balance to the design, but a 2×4 could be used as well.

WRAPPING DECKS AROUND A HOUSE

Decks that wrap around a house offer many benefits, without adding many costs or construction headaches. Turning a corner or two is one of the simplest ways to define separate spaces on a deck. A wraparound deck may allow you to get into or out of the sun or breeze. Or it could create a private nook, separated from the main body of the deck, where you can read or relax in private. It also can offer access to the deck from more than one doorway.

A modest wraparound could include a full-sized deck on one side of the house with a small bump-out on an adjacent side, perhaps to be used for storage. More ambitious decks might surround two or three sides of the house, perhaps on two or more levels. A narrow deck area can function as a walkway. On sloping lots, wraparound decks make moving around the house's perimeter much easier.

ABOVE: *This deck zigzags around the side and back of this home to allow the best view of a nearby river and wetlands.*

BELOW: *This sweeping, rambling deck contains a generous walkway and several areas for lounging and dining, which make it ideal for hosting large parties.*

The expansive deck on this Atlanta home follows not only the ins and outs of the house's exterior but of the landscaping, too. A 200-year-old tree that's the focal point of the yard is enveloped by the deck, adding drama and convenient seating in the shade. Attention to the little things makes all the difference: The latice of the railing on the second-story porch is repeated in the deck's railing, creating an eye-pleasing continuity and making the deck a natural extension of the house. Plenty of glass—in French doors and tall windows all along the back of the house—helps blend indoor and outdoor spaces.

A sweeping view often calls for a deck of sweeping proportions. This house already had an open feel, with plenty of large windows and sliding glass doors facing several directions. A deck on only one side of the house would have looked out of place. This grand walkway now provides an elevated view. When friends gather, they can stroll over the spacious area to take in the view from a number of vantage points. Building a large deck raised this high is a major undertaking and should be planned by a professional deck designer and built by a contractor.

FRAMING A WRAPAROUND DECK

On a wraparound deck you should decide on your decking pattern before you begin framing. The most common solutions are shown here. Each one requires a different framing and foundation plan.

Decking run in two sections perpendicular to each other, *below,* offers a straightforward bit of visual interest and is usually the easiest to build. Decking that turns a corner (*top,* page 79) may be the most attractive, but it is trickier to frame. And laying the decking can be tricky as well, especially if you choose mitered decking. Decking that runs in the same direction (*bottom,* page 79) makes the entire deck look and feel like a unified whole. The framing is a bit unconventional, with joists running parallel to the house on one side and perpendicular to it on the other side. The construction, however, is no more complex than for a basic deck.

Lay out the deck.
Approach the layout for a wraparound deck as though you were building two separate decks. Split the L shape by running a mason's line from the corner of the house to a batter board. In this way, you can ensure each section is square by measuring the diagonals. For this layout, mason's lines mark the centers of posts. Check span charts to determine the proper spacing and sizes for posts, beams, and joists.

Run perpendicular decking.
This wraparound design is essentially two decks set next to each other. The ledger for one section continues beyond the house out to a post, and the parallel beam extends the same distance. At the point where the two sections meet, make sure there is an adequate nailing surface for all decking pieces. Avoid a situation where you need to drive a nail or screw closer than 1 inch from the end of a decking board. Beyond that, framing requirements, such as size and spacing of posts, beams, and joists, can be calculated separately for each section of the deck. This approach works especially well when you want to add a section to an existing deck.

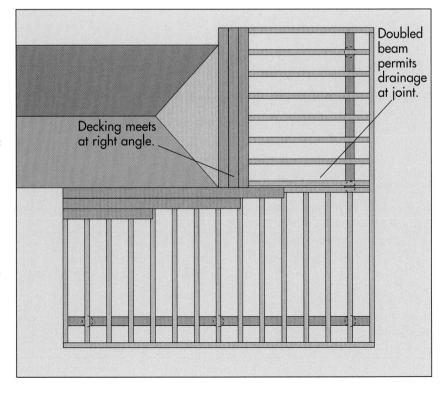

Decking meets at right angle.

Doubled beam permits drainage at joint.

Turn a corner in three ways.

Turning the corner with decking gives a deck a more handcrafted look. But plan carefully, or the point where the decking makes the turn may become a problem spot. Mitered decking is difficult to install because it's hard to keep every joint aligned perfectly. If you first install a decking spacer board along the miter angle, joints won't have to be perfect. A herringbone pattern is the easiest to install and creates a distinctive look.

It is critical that all decking pieces be supported adequately at each end. Doubled joists, with spacer blocks between them, solve this problem. You may not need to use this much lumber, however. For instance, instead of doubling the joists, you might add a 2×4 to each one to increase the nailing surface. You will need to cut many of the joists at a 45-degree bevel and use angled joist hangers.

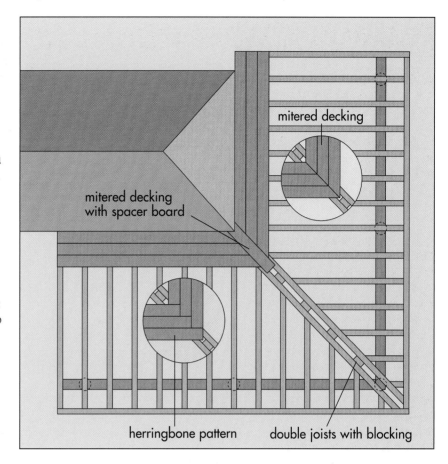

mitered decking

mitered decking with spacer board

herringbone pattern

double joists with blocking

Use a continuous decking pattern.

Another attractive option is to run the decking on both sides of the house in the same direction. This continuity, however, requires a major adjustment in the underlying framing. Install conventional ledgers on both sides of the house. On one side, install a beam that runs the length of the deck. On the other side of the house, install shorter beams, running parallel with the first beam. You can attach these to the house with a second ledger. (Remember, beams must sit below the ledger.) But it may be easier to install footings and posts near the house. Lap the joists over the short beams. Plan ahead for how best to install the decking so joints between boards don't create an irregular pattern at the corner section. Usually, it is best to start with a piece that runs along the house for part of its length.

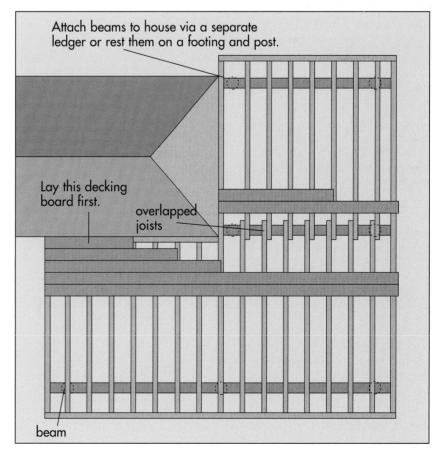

Attach beams to house via a separate ledger or rest them on a footing and post.

Lay this decking board first.

overlapped joists

beam

USING MORE THAN ONE DECK

Decks work well in multiples. A deck that drops down a step or two between levels can break up the monotony of a large deck; it may define separate activity areas on the deck; or it could resolve problems posed by a steep slope, allowing a gradual, stepped decline.

Having more than one deck allows for multiple vantage points for taking in the view, distinct activity areas, and ready access to the outdoors from several rooms.

Nothing about the construction should stop you from considering including more levels or more decks. However, the more complex a design and the more problematic the site, the more desirable the help of a professional designer will be.

ABOVE: Linking decks with multiple landings helps break up an extended stairway and offers alternative activity areas. In this case what could have been a detriment, a deeply sloping yard, is turned into an enticing path to the door surrounded by a green and blooming landscape.

LEFT: A series of small decks step up in bridge-like fashion over natural rock formations to the front of a house. This clever approach allows the house to embrace the rugged site. Additional decks off the side and back of the house allow the homeowners to take in the view from several angles. Keep the terrain in mind as you develop your plan: Steeply sloping sites may require special engineering to meet local building codes.

ABOVE: The home built on this challenging lake-front lot has several decks that serve as yard space. A design this complex is usually designed into the home's construction, but that doesn't preclude adding decks at different levels as part of a renovation.

BELOW: A series of individual decks delightfully march right through the garden and up to the front door. This arrangement allows a maximum appreciation of the landscape with minimal intrusion.

ABOVE: Graceful columns elegantly support the second-story deck, while the matching railings make the visual connection between the spaces. Wrapping from the sunny front to the tree-shaded side of the home, the matching decks take in the full view.

DECK VARIATIONS

Let layout serve all deck levels.
Multilevel decks can be built as a series of independent decks set next to each other. Often, however, a more efficient approach is to let parts of the foundation and framing serve both levels simultaneously. In the example at right, the upper level is constructed as an individual deck. Posts supporting the upper-level beam also support the ledger for the lower level. When building the framing, it often works out well to step levels down by the width of one joist. If you are using 2×8s, that will give you a standard step rise; if you are using 2×6s, you will get a gentle step. The lower level could be expanded or offset by shifting post locations. In this example, the lower level doesn't require a railing, which adds to the distinctiveness of each level.

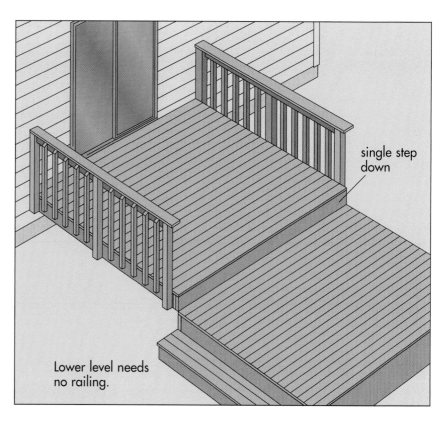

single step down

Lower level needs no railing.

Multilevel decks can be built in stages, as time and finances permit. In this example, the first stage, left, is a basic raised deck, with a generous 4-foot-wide stairway to the yard. The second stage, right, includes a landing a step lower than the first and a ground-level deck surrounding the corner. When the lower levels were added, the original stairs were removed. The salvaged lumber was used to create a slightly narrower stairway between the levels.

Create framing level changes by using stacked boxes, ...

Stacked boxes are an easy way to change levels, but usually are cost efficient only for smaller levels. If the decking runs in the same direction, build the frame so each member rests directly above the underlying frame, as shown. Use toenailed deck screws or mending plates to hold the joists together. If the decking runs in different directions, build a framing box with the joists running in the opposite direction. You can build two modest-sized steps at the doorway with this approach by setting a small box (2×3 feet) on top of a larger box (4×6 feet).

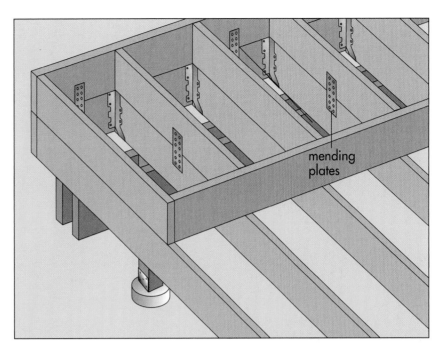

mending plates

using a beam as ledger, ...

To create a one-step level change, often the most efficient technique is to build the upper level so the joists and header joist rest on the beam with no overlap. Attach joist hangers to the beam to carry joists for the lower level. This method can be used to frame a succession of gradual level changes. For a larger height differential between levels, attach a ledger on the outside of the posts and proceed to frame the lower level. Add steps as necessary, perhaps using the stacked boxes method above.

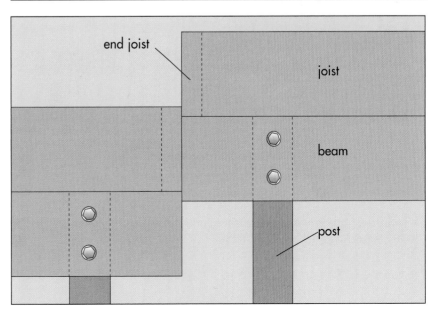

joist hangers

two-piece beam

or building individual decks.

Sometimes it makes the most sense to create level changes by building two or more individual decks. One level could be attached on one end to a ledger on the house, while the other could be freestanding. Each level has its own foundation and framing and is built to the standards required of a single deck. Typically, it's best not to tie the decks together with screws or bolts: Boards will crack and split if one footing settles differently from the other. The best approach often is to build two separate deck levels, then join them together with a set of stairs.

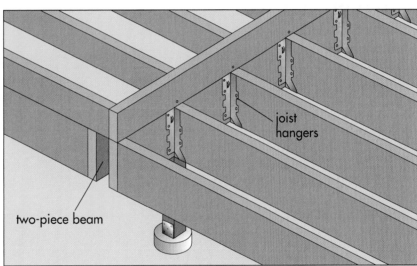

end joist

joist

beam

post

DESIGNING AN ENTRYWAY DECK

Decks are normally thought of as backyard structures built mainly for fun and sun. If you'd like your new deck to function as an entryway as well, consider these design pointers.

The more visible the entryway deck is from the street, the more you want to hide the foundation and framing with lattice or solid skirting. As you design these and other elements, try to integrate the design of the deck with the house by using matching colors or the same siding.

With a well-designed portico roof or other overhead structure, an entryway deck along the front or side of a house can assume a porchlike presence. For entry stairs, consider adding risers and using an enhanced railing design.

ABOVE: Even a simple deck can offer a warm welcome. With the addition of planters, attractive borders, and an entrance-framing awning, this unassuming deck is as hospitable as it is functional. Accessories make a welcoming difference.

BELOW: With basket-weave railing treatment and a wide, tiled stairway, the welcoming graciousness of this old home actually is enhanced by the deck. A far cry from a purely recreational deck, this entryway deck is an extension of the front porch.

RIGHT: The addition of a wide stairway, deep fascia to cover the joists, and lattice skirting seamlessly melds an elegant entry area with space for relaxed entertaining. Add pipe railing, stair risers, and a complementary paint job, and you've transformed a basic deck into a welcoming addition.

BELOW: This graceful, gradually staged entryway deck is made of a series of platforms that ease the ascent to the doorway. The middle platform features a roomy wraparound bench. Metal railings, common to entryways, help establish the deck's front-of-the-house function. Landscaping plays a role too; hidden lights illuminate the pathway at night and tall bushes hide the superstructure of the platforms.

The old concrete steps leading to the front door of this house were cracked, off-kilter, and far from welcoming. A new entryway deck functions like an old-fashioned porch while taming the slope up to the front door. The wide stairs and two landings also offer a place to sit a spell and enjoy the flowers. Although space was tight, the deck doesn't overpower the front of the house. There are some built-in bonuses too, such as a bench for relaxing on the landing, right; a planter for a tree and flowers; and storage underneath the deck for a lawnmower and a couple of bicycles. There is a railing for safety where needed, but the wide stairway is left open for an inviting feel and a clear view. The deck truly is customized to the setting, offering angles and other details. Yet construction is not beyond

the abilities of a moderately experienced do-it-yourselfer. You might want to consider hiring a landscape designer to help draw up the plans and perhaps a contractor to remove the old structure.

EXPERTS' INSIGHT

WHEN A DECK IS NOT A DECK

Tradition says porches belong at the front of houses and decks are for the back. But the differences between a porch and a deck aren't always so clear-cut. On older houses, porches often are enclosed partially and fully integrated into the front facade, often even sharing the roofline of the house. They clearly are extensions of the house rather than afterthoughts. Use construction techniques as you would with a deck, but finish and furnish the new structure as though it were a porch.

CREATING PRIVACY WITH SOLID WALLS

A sure way to integrate an entryway deck with the style of the house is to add solid walls and cover them with siding to match the house. Solid walls are also a great way to add privacy to a backyard deck without giving up its function as an outdoor space. If wind is a problem, a solid wall can offer welcome relief.

The posts supporting a solid wall must be attached firmly to the deck foundation. The siding material will not add significant strength. Usually, an existing deck railing can be modified easily to accept solid siding. Install horizontal rails to handle vertical siding, sheet siding, or plywood backing for shingles.

If you want a semisolid wall, build a standard railing (see pages 54–55) with balusters set close to each other. Or install lattice panels between the deck rails.

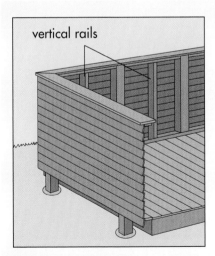

Install horizontal siding, ...
Clapboard or similar horizontal siding can be nailed to vertical rails and posts spaced about 24 inches apart. If you want to match the siding on the house, use the same exposure—the amount of siding width that shows for each board.

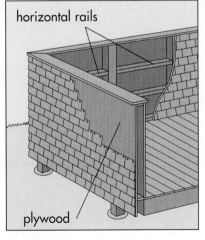

shingles, ...
Shingles on a deck can look great even if the house has a different type of siding. Install horizontal rails no more than 16 inches apart and attach pressure-treated plywood, then the shingles. Paint the shingles, stain and seal them, or just let them weather to gray.

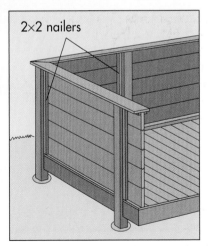

or tongue-and-groove boards.
Solid tongue-and-groove boards look equally attractive from both sides of the deck. Install them centered on the posts with 1×1 or 2×2 nailers on the perimeter, as shown. Or you can nail them to the outside of the posts.

BUILDING FREESTANDING DECKS

A freestanding deck has no connection with the house and, therefore, can be constructed just about anywhere. You can build a freestanding deck adjoining the house, of course, if you don't mind adding a row of footings instead of a ledger board (see page 33). Or you can install the deck in a remote part of the yard to take advantage of a great view or to add to its privacy. Use a series of freestanding decks built at different levels to create a gradual stairway.

A modular deck (pages 89–91) is the simplest of freestanding decks and needs no foundation. In fact, a freestanding deck may not need the substantial footings required for attached decks. If the footings for an attached deck do not extend below the frostline, boards could crack in the winter because the footings will rise up and the ledger will not. But a freestanding deck with footings above the frostline is in no such danger—all the footings will rise and fall together.

EXPERTS' INSIGHT

REASONS FOR A FREESTANDING DECK

In areas where the soil is unstable, deck builders usually build freestanding decks to avoid problems due to uneven settling. Many deck contractors throughout the country build all their decks unattached to the house because ledger boards trap moisture, which can lead to rot in the deck and in the house structure. Digging and pouring a few more footings actually may be less work than installing a ledger board.

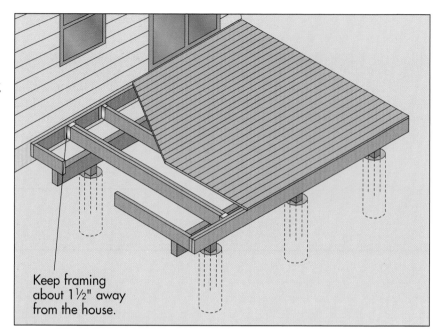

Keep framing about 1½" away from the house.

Create an independent foundation.
An elevated freestanding deck can be built following standard deck-building procedures. Instead of tying into the house's foundation through a ledger, however, a freestanding deck requires its own independent foundation. On a simple rectangular design, this requires that you double the number of footings and attach a beam on each row of posts.

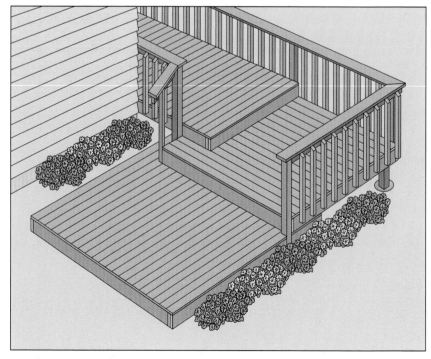

Combine attached and freestanding deck areas.
By setting a substantial part of a deck so it is separated clearly from the house, the transition from house to yard becomes more graceful. The lower portion of the above deck is separated from the house just enough to leave room for an attractive flower bed.

CREATING MODULAR DECKING

These simple structures, often called duckboards, are easy to build, and they can be combined into a myriad of shapes with an attractive parquet design. If you have a level yard and soil that is not soggy, they can last a long time. If you lay them on a firmly tamped bed of gravel, they will remain fairly stable.

If you are going to use modular decking in high-traffic areas or find the modules have more spring to the step than you'd prefer, add a 2×4 cleat to the center of each module as reinforcement.

YOU'LL NEED

TIME: 1 hour to build the jig and about 1 hour for each module.
SKILLS: Measuring, cutting, fastening with nails or screws.
TOOLS: Basic carpentry tools.

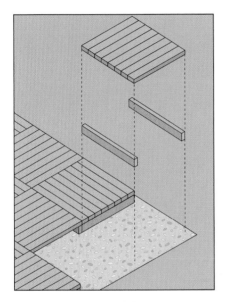

Combine basic modules.
A modular deck can be constructed in a weekend and installed on any level surface in your yard. It requires no connection to the house and no foundation. Add or subtract modules to suit your needs.

Mix and match modules.
With a bit of creativity, you may be able to think of several ways to combine modular construction with standard deck-building techniques. For example, here the modules form a path from the garage to the deck. If your needs or traffic patterns change over the years, it is a simple matter to pick up and rearrange the modules. You can even stack them to make low steps. Alternate the direction of the decking for a parquet effect, as shown, or lay them so the decking lines are continuous.

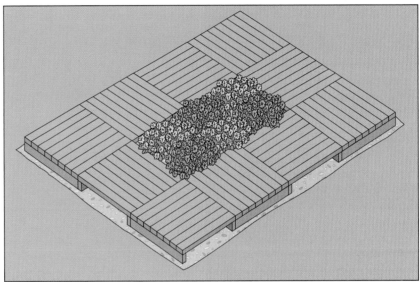

Add units to form any pattern.
Modular construction, by its nature, is versatile and adaptable. You can use the modular approach, for example, to build a large border around a flower bed. A larger deck could encompass several individual beds. The modular approach works particularly well for raised gardening beds. For noninvasive plants, simply arrange the modules around an open space. For larger plants or for a raised bed, build a simple planter box and butt the modules up to it.

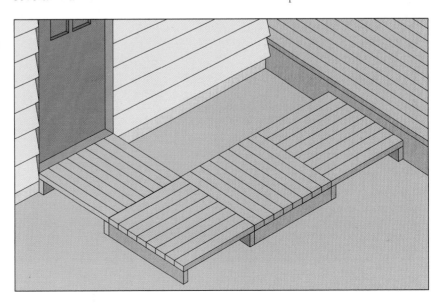

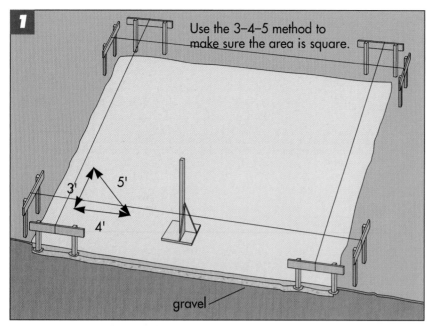

Use the 3–4–5 method to make sure the area is square.

3' 5' 4'

gravel

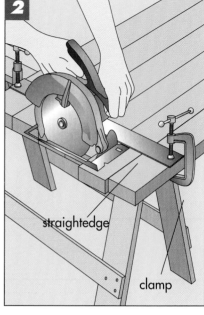

straightedge

clamp

1. Prepare the site.

Use batter boards and mason's lines to mark the outline of the area. Allow for a 3-inch border of sand around the perimeter of the deck. Use the 3–4–5 method (see page 40) to ensure a square layout. Remove the sod and soil to a depth of 5 inches (or more or less, depending on how high you want the deck to sit). Spread 3 inches of gravel on the ground, level and tamp it, then add 1½ inches of sand. Level and tamp again. For an extra-firm surface, rent a vibrating tamper.

2. Gang cut the boards.

For each module, you need ten 29-inch pieces of pressure-treated 2×4s. Make the job go faster by setting several 2×4s edge to edge on sawhorses, then cutting them in one pass with a circular saw. Use a straightedge to clamp the boards and guide the saw.

Money $ Saver

SAVE THE SOD

The sod and topsoil you remove to make room for your deck can be added to your compost pile. Be sure to place the grass side down to stop the grass from growing.

Before you do so, however, think about some other uses you may have for it. Perhaps part of your yard would benefit from transplanted sod—an out-of-use garden bed might need just such a boost. Use a straight-bladed shovel and cut the sod in careful rectangles to pull up sections of sod that can be laid out easily in another location. Be sure to pull up as many of the roots as possible as you work.

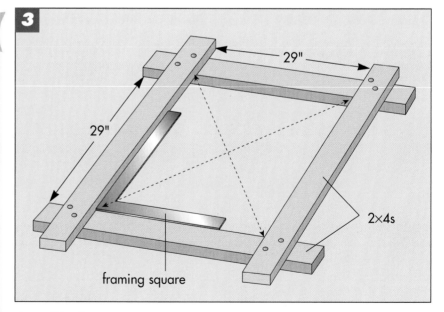

29"

29"

2×4s

framing square

3. Build a jig.

To ensure each module is identical and perfectly square, make this jig out of 2×4s. Use four boards, each about 3 to 4 feet long. Make sure the inside edges are straight and measure 29×29 inches. Align the corners with a framing square before nailing the boards together. Use several nails at each corner. The jig doesn't have cross bracing, so be sure to check it for square from time to time.

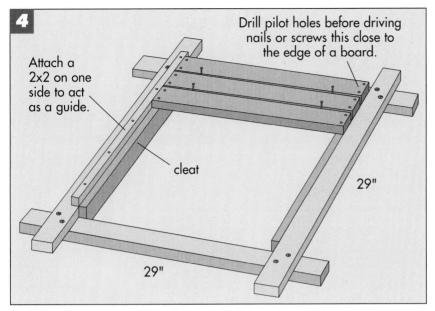

4

Drill pilot holes before driving nails or screws this close to the edge of a board.

Attach a 2x2 on one side to act as a guide.

cleat

29"

29"

5

Drive nails through cleats

4. Build the modules.

Set the jig on a solid, flat surface, such as a concrete driveway. Each module requires eight decking pieces and two bottom cleats. Set two boards on end at opposite sides of the jig, as shown, to act as nailing cleats. Attach the rest of the boards with 12d galvanized nails or 2½-inch decking screws. Space the boards with the 12d nails, making a ⅛-inch gap between boards. You may need to adjust the spacing to make the last piece come out even with the end of the cleats.

5. Set the modules.

Lay the modules in place, alternating the direction of the boards if you want a parquet effect. Attach the modules to each other by drilling pilot holes and driving in galvanized nails or screws at an angle.

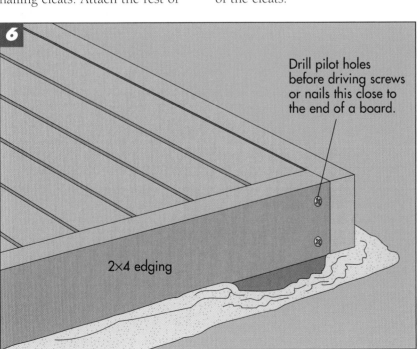

6

Drill pilot holes before driving screws or nails this close to the end of a board.

2×4 edging

6. Add the edging.

Once you have assembled the modules in a pattern, you may want to install 2×4s around the edges of the deck to add a finishing touch. Cut two 2×4s to fit flush with the decking and install them on opposite ends. Remove enough sand to allow the edging to rest flush with the deck surface. Then cut two more 2×4s long enough to overlap the ends of the installed edging. Replace the sand and tamp around the edges.

EXPERTS' INSIGHT

WOOD PATH

These simple modules can serve another function. Set them end to end to form a wood path or sidewalk. The modules are considerably easier to build and install than a concrete walkway or a brick sidewalk. Use the wood path to connect the house to the garage, or the house to a freestanding deck. Use the jig shown above left to build a 29-inch-wide path, or adjust the size of the jig for a narrower version. With a bit of excavation, the modules could be set to rest at grade. In areas with cold climates, it may make sense to store the modules in the garage during the winter.

USING DECKS AS POOL OR SPA SURROUNDS

A wood surface looks great next to water. A well-built deck adds comfort and safety and will withstand years of use in its wet surroundings if maintained properly (see page 105). A pool or hot-tub surround can be part of a larger deck complex. Use level changes or privacy walls to isolate this part of the deck. A deck can facilitate access to the water while masking the less attractive profile of a pool or hot tub.

Pools and hot tubs require plumbing and electrical connections, which can be hidden or at least obscured by the deck's framing. It is important, however, to allow easy access to these spaces, either from beneath the deck or through a removable door on the surface.

Many municipalities have strict requirements for fencing around pools and hot tubs. With careful planning you may be able to combine the required fencing with a railing system on a deck.

A pool or hot-tub surround built as a deck is also an easy way to create additional recreation space, especially when the ground slopes down and away from the pool. If possible, build the deck while the pool is empty to avoid the danger of operating power tools around water.

CHOOSING LUMBER

Be sure to select high-quality wood whenever you build near water. It must be highly rot resistant, of course, because it will get wet often. The wood should be smooth and splinter-free, also, so people will feel comfortable sitting on it with bare legs. Heartwood of cedar or redwood are the best choices, but #1 grade pressure-treated lumber may be okay.

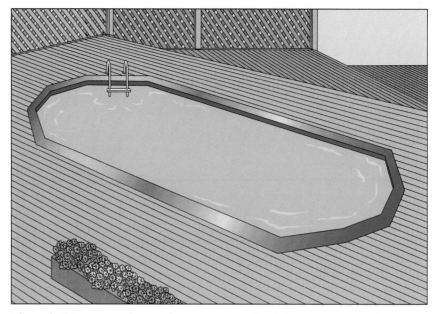

Place decking around a pool.
Though it is usual to have a tile or concrete surface around an in-ground swimming pool, a wood surface looks great and is more comfortable. Swimmers who emerge from the water to sunbathe will find the warmth of the decking welcoming.

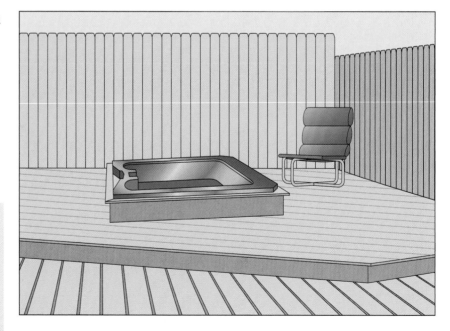

Raise a spa off a deck.
When designing a deck around a whirlpool or hot tub, decide whether it is more important to have a nice wooden surface to sit on while you dangle your feet in the water or to get in and out of the spa easily. Here, the spa itself supplies an ample seating area, and the owners decided that ease of entry and exit from the pool was more important. So they raised the spa up about 14 inches above the deck.

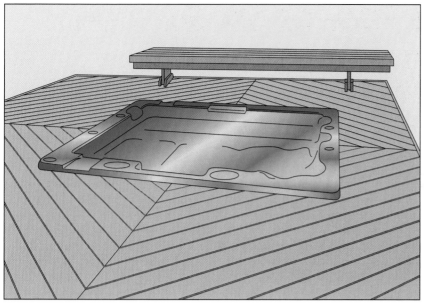

Set a spa flush with the deck.

In this design, the spa's rim rests on top of the decking, making it easy for bathers to sit on the deck surface with their feet in the water. Do not use the spa's rim to bear the weight of the spa; it must be supported from beneath. (See sidebar at right.) Safety is especially important with this design because small children, or even adults, easily can fall in accidentally. Always place a sturdy cover over a spa when not in use.

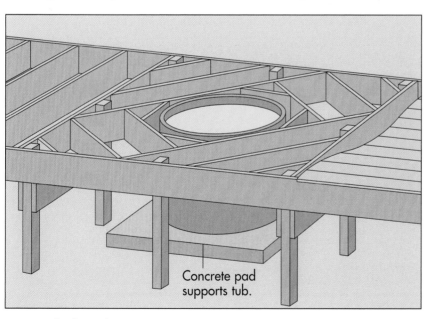

Concrete pad supports tub.

Surround a hot tub.

Your hot tub or spa should rest on a solid, level surface, ideally a steel-reinforced concrete pad that sits on undisturbed soil. A water-and-people-filled hot tub can weigh several thousand pounds, so the deck should not carry any of the load. The deck plan shown here provides framing that rises an inch or so above the top of the tub. Install the decking by running it "wild" over the surface of the tub, then cutting out a circle with a sabersaw. Thoroughly router and sand the cut edges so you have a smooth, splinter-free place on which to sit.

SUPPORTING A SPA OR HOT TUB

All that water in a spa or hot tub can weigh plenty, so be sure to provide a solid surface for it to rest on. Begin by checking local building codes. Most call for a foundation of steel-reinforced concrete resting on undisturbed soil. Codes also may require footings that extend below the frostline; but if you drain the tub in the winter, that may not be necessary. In some nonfreezing areas, the "washed sand" technique is common: Temporarily suspend a spa about a foot above the bottom of a hole. Pour in sand below the spa and thoroughly soak it with water. Repeat the process until the cavity under the tub is filled.

EXPERTS' INSIGHT

SAFETY UNDERFOOT

It's not just the area directly around the tub that needs to be splinter-free. The entire deck surrounding a pool or hot tub will receive a lot of barefooted traffic. Take extra steps to minimize the chance of splinters or other sharp edges coming in contact with those feet. Buy the best grade of decking material you can afford. Decking with rounded edges and pretreated with sealer is a good choice. Be sure to replace nails or screws that start to pop up (see page 107). Plan on resealing the wood at least twice annually to protect it from moisture. Sweep the area regularly to keep twigs and stones off the surface.

SURROUNDING IN-GROUND POOLS

If you are planning to install a new in-ground pool, consider a deck surround as an elegant alternative to flagstones or other masonry materials. Decking for an in-ground pool could cover the entire perimeter. But you can combine materials so people have their choice of wood or masonry to walk or lounge on. On hot days, a light-colored tile can provide a cool spot, while on most days people will prefer the warmth of natural wood.

If you have an existing pool surrounded by an aging concrete platform, a new deck surround can be built directly on top of the concrete, as long as it is still basically strong. If the concrete is loose and unstable, however, hire a contractor to remove it—not as big a job as it may sound, but one that requires heavy-duty trucks and strong backs.

Custom-fit deck to the pool shape.
If there is no existing concrete surface, build right up to the edge of the pool by extending joists along the perimeter, then cutting the decking to fit the pool shape perfectly. If the area around the pool is open ground, use standard footings and piers to support the deck surround.

Place decking over concrete.
You can place a deck right on top of a existing concrete surround. The concrete can serve as the foundation as long as it is in relatively sound condition. Install pressure-treated 2×4 or 2×3 sleepers on the patio. Space them like joists on a regular deck, and fasten them to the concrete using masonry screws. Drill pilot holes through the sleepers, then mark for the locations of the holes in the concrete. Drill the holes with a masonry bit, reposition the sleeper, and drive in the masonry screws. You'll need a heavy-duty drill and extra masonry bits. Use short sleepers to snake along irregularly shaped edges. Leave gaps between the sleepers along the perimeter to facilitate drainage. Use pressure-treated shims to fill in low spots between the sleepers and concrete.

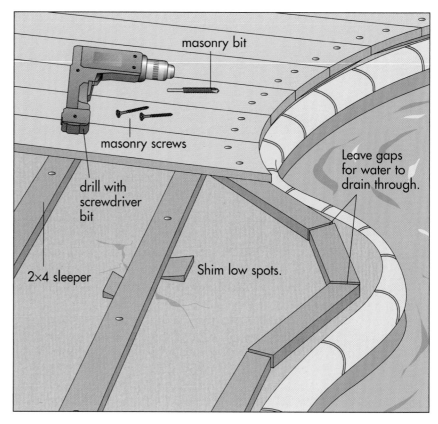

SURROUNDING ABOVE-GROUND POOLS

Above-ground pools are less expensive than in-ground pools. As much as manufacturers try, however, these pools tend to be ugly. A raised deck surrounding the pool can offset its bold presence somewhat by offering a more graceful transition between surfaces. A deck can provide more of the appearance and convenience of an in-ground pool. It also hides and protect the pool's plumbing and filtering equipment.

A deck surround makes the pool easier to use and, thus, more fun. Make the platform large enough for patio furniture, so you can sunbathe and perhaps dine between dips.

If possible, use a deck to connect the pool with the house entrance. In most cases, this will require some level changes to account for the different heights of the pool and doorway. Otherwise, build a free-standing structure with a set of stairs.

Keep decking and framing 1 inch or so away from the pool at all points.

bracing

Take the plunge.
One of the challenges of building a deck around an above-ground pool is to provide safe access to the edge of the pool while keeping the deck structurally separate. Use bracing for added support against swaying. Decide whether you want the decking to be below or above the level of the pool's rim and keep wood surfaces about an inch away from the pool.

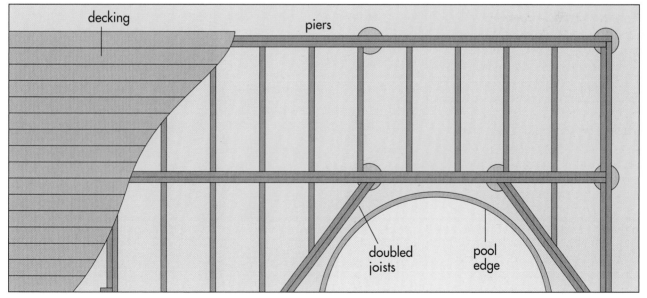

decking

piers

doubled joists

pool edge

Develop a framing plan.
A common approach to framing a pool surround is to place footings and posts around the perimeter of the pool, spaced at even intervals around the curved parts. Then attach doubled joists to the beams so at all points they come close enough to the pool to support decking hanging over the pool. You may need to fill in some places with short, bevel-cut joists. Run the other joists up to the doubled joists. Some pieces must be cut at odd bevels. Build the rest of the framing as you would a standard deck. Install the decking so it overhangs the edge of the pool, then cut the decking to match the arc of the pool. Sand all the curve-cut edges smooth.

DESIGNING ELEVATED DECKS

People build houses on steep slopes because they offer spectacular views and often because the sites can be purchased at bargain rates. The trade-off, however, may be a largely unusable yard. One way to make the most of the situation is to build a deck over the elevation. An elevated deck stands on posts to reach the main level of the house or to flatten a sloping site, which often is expensive or impractical to flatten or terrace.

With split-level and other house designs that have elevated floors, traditional masonry patios are too far below indoor living spaces. An elevated deck can solve this problem as well.

Fortunately, a deck can rise to nearly any height, reaching a second story or even higher. For example, an elevated design can provide a private sun deck or balcony off an upstairs bedroom and be connected to the room with a new door.

Footing requirements for a raised deck may be extremely stringent, especially if your site slopes severely. Hire a professional contractor to dig the holes with a truck-mounted auger bore.

A straightforward raised deck may require large posts and visible framing, which might not be the look you're after. You may be able to soften the effect by stepping down with a series of small deck areas or large stairways. In this case, the homeowner did just that to connect the house with a patio area that sits far below the house.

If you build an elevated deck, it often makes sense to build an intermediate-level deck at the same time, even if you will not be building a stairway down to the ground. The lower deck shares the same footings and posts as the upper deck so it will be relatively inexpensive to build. In this example, the lower deck is screened in for insect-free use and the upper deck is used on pleasant days.

CAUTION!
HIGH POSTS, IRREGULAR PIERS
Raised decks can be difficult and even dangerous to build. Posts and beams often must be made of heavy, large-dimension lumber. Working up in the air can be tricky as well as tedious. Tackle such a job yourself only if you are confident of your skills, have good help, and are equipped with strong ladders or scaffolding. Get advice from a professional on the footings before proceeding.

Small raised decks can function as balconies. While not suitable for a family dining area or large parties, balconies offer a private area for a person to read or sunbathe or a spot where two or three people can gather to converse and enjoy the view. This family chose to build not just one balcony deck but four. In that way, every member of the family has easy access, via a bedroom or the family room, to a cozy spot with a great view. On a site this steep, extending the decks outward would have meant a great deal of expense. Three of the balconies use standard posts, and the fourth is a rooftop deck.

On this lakefront home, a straightforward stairway from the elevated deck would have reached too far into the yard and made the house look nearly like a public place, open to the beach below. By running the walkway in three directions—first a stairway alongside the house, then a path out from the house, then another stairway alongside the house in the opposite direction—the homeowners gained the feel of a spiral stairway. The stairway leading to the ground is clearly private, hidden from the beach by the octagonal shape of the lower level, which also enhances the sense of circularity. Three modest-sized deck areas define an upper balcony, a dining area, and a conversation pit with a built-in bench. The hot tub also was located so as to limit its visibility from the beach.

How High Can You Go?

Maximum Post Height, Based on Load Area
(beam spacing × post spacing, in square feet)

Post Size	36	48	60	72	84	96	108	120
4×4	10'	9'	8'	7'	6'	5'		
4×6	14'	12'	11'	10'	9'	8'	7'	
6×6	17'	16'	15'	14'	13'	12'		

This table presents standard height limitations for Southern pine and Douglas fir (graded #2 and better), the most commonly available species of pressure-treated lumber. To determine an acceptable post length for your deck, figure the "load area." Multiply the joist span (in feet) by the beam span (in feet) to determine the load area (in square feet). The joist span is defined as the spacing between beams or between the beam and ledger; the beam span equals the distance between posts.

For example, if your deck has joists spanning 8 feet and a beam spanning 6 feet, the load area on the deck equals 48. Look under the appropriate column in the table and you will find you can use 4×4 posts up to 9 feet long. If your deck has a higher elevation, use bigger posts. (See page 30 for more on joist and beam spans.)

The above figures will be acceptable under most building codes, but always check your local codes before starting work. Of course, you can always use larger posts than are required. On elevated decks, 6×6 posts often look better than 4×4s, even if they aren't needed.

EXPERTS' INSIGHT

SAFE HEIGHTS

■ The maximum acceptable length of posts that you can use on a given deck depends on several factors, including the size of the post, wood species and quality, the sizes and spans of joists and beams, and local building codes and regulations.

■ Higher decks require larger posts spaced closer together and resting on larger foundations.

■ If the posts on your deck also will support a substantial overhead structure, check with a professional or your local building department officials about the best size to use.

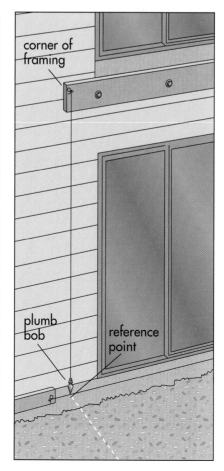

corner of framing

plumb bob

reference point

Locate the footings.

It's crucial to locate footings correctly so the posts they support will be exactly plumb as they reach far upward to support an elevated deck. Begin by accurately locating a reference point for the entire framing structure.

The easiest way is to install the ledger board, then hang a plumb bob from the corner. This identifies the location of the corner of the framing, so make the correct calculations to figure the true reference point for the footings.

To lay out the actual location of the first footing, use the 3–4–5 method (see page 40) to extend a mason's line out from the house at exactly 90 degrees. If your property slopes, have a helper hold a board with a level on it, with its end resting on the ground where the footing will be. When the outward measurement is correct and the board is plumb in both directions, you will have the correct location.

BRACING TALL POSTS

Building codes often require decks with posts taller than 6 feet to have lateral bracing. Your local code will dictate if deck posts must be braced. Most bracing can be made with 2×4s; but for braces more than 8 feet long, use 2×6s. Secure braces with ⅜-inch lag screws with washers or carriage bolts with nuts and washers.

Freestanding decks should be braced if they are more than 3 feet above ground. Decks that may be exposed to earthquakes, high winds, or especially heavy loads have stricter bracing requirements. Although it may not be required, bracing strengthens any deck, with little extra time and expense. Solid skirting or a high-quality lattice may be able to take the place of bracing under some codes.

EXPERTS' INSIGHT

BRACING FOR DISASTER

Bracing is one construction practice that nonprofessionals sometimes don't understand and, thus, too often overlook. The posts on elevated decks, just like the walls of most framed houses, must be secured laterally to resist climatic and load forces. Without bracing, excessive winds against the side of a house could cause the walls to sag. On most houses, the bracing is provided by sheathing. But most decks don't have sheathing, so additional bracing is necessary to keep the posts from swaying. The taller the posts, the more important the bracing is to the structure.

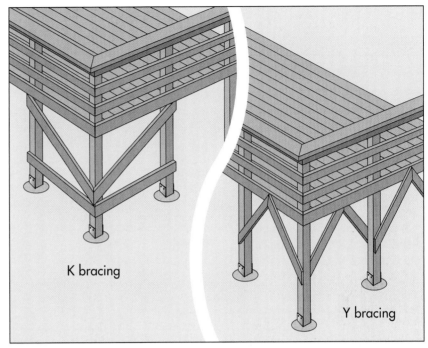

K bracing

Y bracing

Brace decks between posts.
Bracing styles are often named after the letters they form. The most common types are K and Y, *above,* and X and W, *below.* The strongest bracing ties posts to beams. Post-to-post braces usually must be longer because they must span from one post to the next. The style of bracing you use may depend on how accessible you want the space beneath the deck to be.

To prevent rot and give the braces a neater appearance, angle the end cuts so each end is vertical when the brace is installed. When two braces meet on a post, leave a small gap between them to allow for drainage.

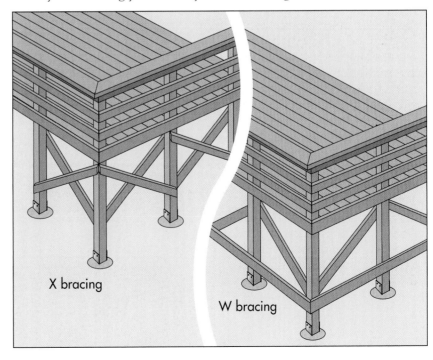

X bracing

W bracing

SELECTING FINISHES

Even the best-built decks can't escape weathering. In nearly every case, it is a good idea to apply a protective finish to wood surfaces. Coat the entire deck with a wood finish soon after you finish building it. To get the color you want, perhaps to complement your house, use an exterior stain. Even if you want a weathered look, don't simply let nature take its toll; finishes are available that protect the wood while allowing it to age in appearance.

Pressure-treated wood must be finished just like every other type of wood. It should be coated with a water repellent and regularly maintained with finishes that help restore the preservatives in the wood. Redwood and cedar also need protection, especially if they contain light-colored sapwood. Penetrating finishes soak in, while film-forming finishes sit on the surface of the wood.

The elements are wood's enemies.
The sun's ultraviolet rays penetrate the wood less than $1/64$ of an inch, causing only cosmetic damage. But cycles of wetting and drying cause wood to expand and contract, leading to cracking, cupping, and warping. If wood stays moist for a long time, fungus can grow, rotting the wood or producing ugly black mildew. Insects may also be a problem; if they attack houses in your area, expect them to attack your deck.

Stain pressure-treated lumber.
If you use pressure-treated lumber, you don't have to live with that greenish yellow or dirty gray color. By letting the wood dry a bit and applying special stains, you can approximate the look of redwood or cedar. You may need to apply two coats of stain. The bleachlike stain shown on the right-hand board, *above,* simply was brushed on. For a bit more expense you can buy brown pressure-treated lumber that looks similar to redwood; however, it needs to be restained regularly.

DON'T WAIT
A rule of thumb formerly was to let your deck dry out under the hot sun for months before applying a finish. Some suppliers of finishes and lumber continue to offer this advice. Don't listen to them. The most important coat of finish your deck receives will be the first one. For a new deck built with pressure-treated lumber, let the decking dry out about two to four weeks, depending on weather conditions. Test the lumber for dryness by sprinkling water on the surface. If it soaks in readily, the surface is ready to receive a finish. Untreated lumber should be finished as soon as it is dry to the touch. If you wait too long, the surface of the wood will have begun to degrade already.

Use a penetrating finish.

The most common types of penetrating finishes are water repellents, water repellents with preservatives, and semitransparent stains. Water repellents are transparent, protecting the wood from water damage without altering its natural coloration. Water repellents with an added preservative also combat mildew.

Ultraviolet (UV) stabilizers are additives used in some clear finishes that offer some protection from sun damage. Semitransparent stains are more durable than water repellents. The pigments used in the stain protect better against sun damage. In addition, penetrating finishes can include an insecticide. Look for products specifically made for use on decks.

EXPERTS' INSIGHT

WATCH YOUR VOCs

Wood finishes of all kinds have undergone drastic changes in recent years. In an effort to clean up the air, many states have passed legislation requiring manufacturers to reduce the volatile organic compounds (VOCs) in finishes. VOCs are the materials in the finish that evaporate as the finish cures. VOCs from wood finishes, especially from solvent-borne (oil-based) ones, have been found to be significant pollutants. Now, low-VOC finishes are available. Water-borne finishes, such as latex paint or stain, have been affected to a lesser degree by the regulations because water is the principal evaporator. These new products generally do not last as long as oil-based finishes.

Use film-forming finishes sparingly.

Film-forming finishes protect wood by creating a solid barrier (film) on the surface. Paint, solid-color stain, lacquer, and varnish are examples of film-forming finishes. None of these products is recommended for use on decking. Varnish and lacquer do not hold up well under sun and rain. Solid color stains weather quickly on horizontal surfaces and are difficult to repair once they fail. Paint offers great protection against water and ultraviolet light, but virtually no protection against mildew. If you want to paint your deck to enhance its appearance, consider painting only the more visible, especially vertical, parts, such as posts and railings. Coat the wood first with a water repellent preservative and liberally prime the end grain before brushing on the paint.

INGREDIENTS IN DECK FINISHES

Ingredient	Description	Uses	Comments
Water repellent	Wax, usually paraffin, suspended in a binder	Prevents water from soaking into the wood	Easy to apply, but requires annual or biannual applications
Preservatives	Typically include a mildewcide, sometimes an insecticide	Prevents fungi, especially mildew, from growing on the wood; repels insects, such as termites	Should be used regularly on most decks in most parts of the country
UV stabilizers	Reduce degradation of wood due to ultraviolet radiation	Frequently added to clear finishes	Generally not as effective as pigment in preventing UV damage
Pigment	Ingredient or ingredients that give color to the finish	Found in paint, solid-color stain, and semitransparent stain	Protects well against UV and water damage, but ages quickly on decks

GETTING THE LOOK YOU WANT

The Wet Look. To get a long-lasting glossy finish that makes your deck always look like it's just rained, you need to spend extra money and exert extra effort. Buy an alkyd resin product made for your type of wood and your conditions. Some of these products do not work well, however, if the deck stays wet for long periods. You will need to apply it in a two-step process.

As Close to the Original Look of the Wood as Possible. Use a transparent stain containing a UV (ultraviolet ray) stabilizer or blocker. It actually contains a bit of pigment—there's no other way to block out the effects of the sun—which will change the color of the wood slightly. If you don't use a product with UV protection, the sun eventually will change the wood's color much more dramatically.

Silvery Gray. If you use high-quality redwood or cedar, composed entirely of dark-colored heartwood (as opposed to cream-colored sapwood) and leave it untreated, the wood will turn a softly shining gray. By doing nothing, however, you run the risk of cracking and splintering because the wood is not protected from wet-and-dry cycles. If you use a clear product containing water repellent, the wood will turn gray without the cracking. If you let pressure-treated lumber go untreated, it will turn a dirty, not a silvery, gray.

Removing the Gray. If your deck already has turned gray and you don't like it, wash it with wood bleach or fungicide (the color actually is caused by a thin layer of mildew). This will not bring back the original color of the wood, but it will give you a bleached wood that can be stained to the color of your choice.

CHOOSING FINISHING TOOLS

Most deck finishes can be applied with a brush, pad, roller, or sprayer. Paint stores sell inexpensive pump sprayers similar to those used by gardeners. Rollers and sprayers are quick, but wood will absorb more finish, thus protecting it better, if the finish is worked in with a brush. Brushing especially is recommended for the first coat of finish on a new deck.

An efficient and effective technique for applying finish is to work with a partner. One person uses a sprayer or roller to apply the finish to the wood, while the other follows closely behind to work the finish into the wood with a brush.

Be sure to use the right brush for the type of finish you are applying. Natural bristle brushes usually are recommended for solvent-based (oil-based) finishes; synthetic brushes are better for water-borne finishes.

WHEN TO RECOAT

If your deck is finished with a water repellent, it should be recoated at least once a year. Semitransparent stains should require recoating every two to three years. But these are general rules. Decks in different climate regions treated with different finishes may require extremely different refinishing schedules. You can tell when a semitransparent stain has begun to age by comparing how much color has worn away. A good test for checking the condition of a water repellent is to sprinkle water on a dry deck. If the wood quickly soaks up the water, it should be recoated soon. If the water beads up, you can assume safely that the deck doesn't need a new finish yet.

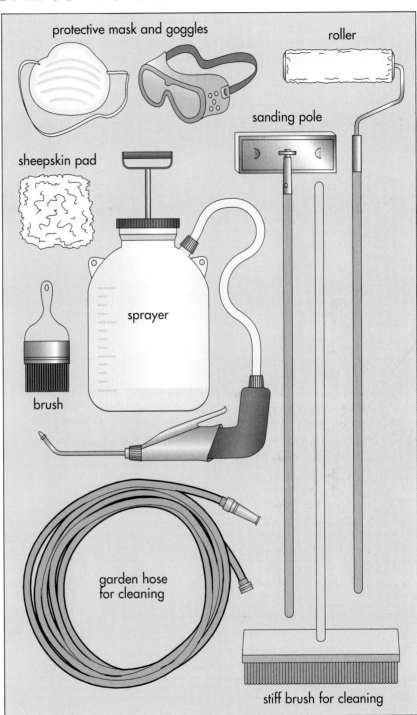

protective mask and goggles

roller

sanding pole

sheepskin pad

sprayer

brush

garden hose for cleaning

stiff brush for cleaning

APPLYING DECK FINISHES

Manufacturers of paints, stains, and repellents make frequent adjustments in the contents of their products, and application instructions change as well. So always read the label and follow instructions carefully. Many companies have toll-free numbers for answers to technical questions. Your local supplier also should be a source of advice on which product to use and how to get the best results from the finish.

The most important coat of deck finish is the first one, so take extra care with a new deck. The moisture content of the wood should be less than 20 percent, and preferably closer to 12 percent in most climates. You may be able to rent or borrow a moisture meter if you'd like to know for sure. Redwood and cedar generally can be finished if the surface feels dry. Pressure-treated lumber often can look dry yet still be wet internally; wait about two to four weeks, depending on weather conditions, before applying finish to treated wood. If the wood easily soaks up a bit of water sprinkled on it, it is ready to finish.

For best results, clean and lightly sand the deck before applying a finish. Wait for a dry, but slightly overcast day—too much sun will dry the finish before it has a chance to soak into the wood.

YOU'LL NEED

TIME: About 4 hours for an average deck.
SKILLS: No special skills, just read and follow instructions.
TOOLS: Brush, goggles; optional application tools include sprayer, roller, or pad.

1. Sand the surface.
Before applying finish on a new deck, sand the wood with 120-grit sandpaper to roughen the surface and encourage absorption. Use a sanding pole to speed up the sanding and save your back. This should take less than an hour for a medium-size deck.

2. Clean off dust and dirt.
A clean deck absorbs a finish better than a dirty one. Sweep it thoroughly, rinse with a hose, and let the deck dry. If your deck already is showing signs of age, scrub it with a chlorine bleach solution or deck cleaner.

3. Apply the finish.
To prevent lap marks, maintain a "wet edge"; that is, don't let the finish dry in an area before you overlap it with wet finish. This is particularly important with pigmented finishes. If you use a roller or sprayer, have a helper follow right behind you to work the finish into the wood with a brush before it dries.

4. Recoat if required.
Read and follow the instructions on the label. Some clear deck finishes require application of a second coat before the first coat dries. Always apply an extra coat or two to exposed end grain. Semitransparent stains often require only a single coat; additional coats result in excessive color or visible brush marks.

MAINTAINING AND TROUBLESHOOTING DECKS

Good construction techniques, high-quality materials, and regular maintenance add many years to the life of a deck. You should pay close attention to the following five major weak areas:

- At and just above ground level.
- Areas where water is likely to be trapped.
- Board ends (exposed end grain).
- Anywhere wood touches wood.
- Sections of wood that have been notched.

By finding and repairing problems early, you can avoid big and expensive repairs down the road. Do a thorough inspection of your deck at least once a year. If possible, inspect beneath the deck's surface. If your deck is too close to the ground to allow you to crawl beneath it, remove some decking boards so you can get a good look.

You'll be looking for soft spots, indicating rot. Do this simply by poking the wood with a screwdriver or awl. If you find part of the deck seems to be in worse condition than other parts, try to find the source of the problem before attempting a repair. Perhaps water damage is occurring in one spot because of faulty gutters or the accumulation of leaves or dirt.

If you find potentially serious problems at the ledger, posts, beams, or joists, consult a professional. Most components of a deck can be repaired or replaced, but repairing some elements are trickier than others.

YOU'LL NEED

TIME: An annual inspection should take 1 to 2 hours.
SKILLS: Diagnosing rotting wood and analyzing potential structural failures.
TOOLS: Flashlight, screwdriver or awl, basic carpentry tools for repairs.

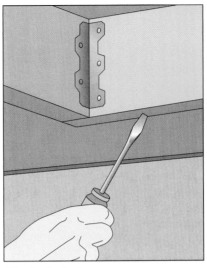

Check the ledger.
The connection between the deck and the house is particularly critical. Check that flashing is in good condition. Use a probe to inspect for water damage on the ledger. Check for bodies of fungi, blue or black stains, and little piles of sawdust indicating the presence of termites or carpenter ants. Tighten all fasteners.

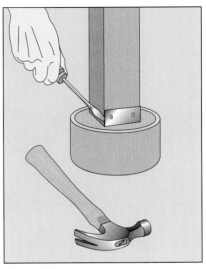

Check the posts.
Check posts most carefully at the ground line and at the top. Use a probe to inspect for rot by sticking it into various parts of the post and comparing the ease of penetration. Try to assess the internal condition—posts often decay from the inside out. Inspect and secure the post's connection with the foundation.

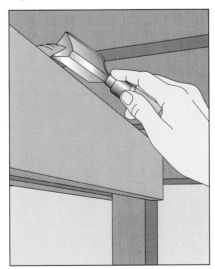

Check beams and joists.
Use a probe around the ends of joists, where they are most prone to rot. If joists sit on top of a beam, check the contact spots. Inspect the connection between the beams and posts. Determine if any joists seem to be slow in drying out.

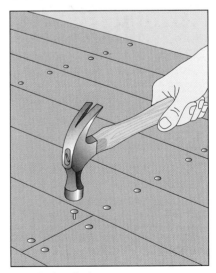

Check the decking.
This is the easiest part to inspect. Pay special attention to the ends of boards and areas around and under butt joints. Tighten nails or screws in the decking and replace badly damaged boards. Inspect for rot where the decking boards meet the joists.

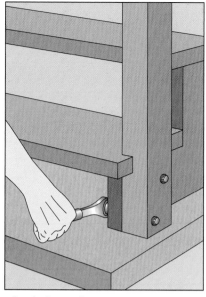

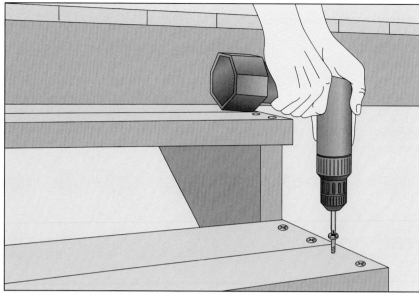

Check the railing.

Railings, and especially stair rails, often are subject to extra strain. Inspect posts for signs of damage and make sure all fasteners are secure and tight. Look at the ends of all rails for water damage. Replace broken balusters.

Check stringers and treads.

Inspect stringers for splits or rot, especially around areas in contact with treads and other wood. The cut portions of stringers have exposed end grain, some portions of which face upward and can collect water; this is a very common problem area. Check the top and bottom connections of stringers. Tighten railing posts and replace damaged treads. If a tread has cupped so it now collects a small puddle of water when it rains, turn it upside-down or replace it.

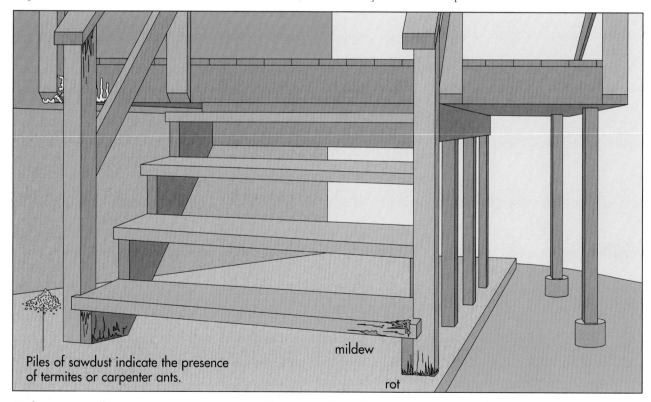

Piles of sawdust indicate the presence of termites or carpenter ants.

mildew

rot

Make an overall assessment.

Make an assessment of your total deck by looking for potential problems besides rot. Check that everything is still plumb and level, especially posts, whose footings may have settled. Small piles of sawdust or tunnels following the grain of wood indicate wood-eating insects. Black slime indicates the presence of mildew (see page 107). If fasteners are causing rust stains on the wood, replace them. Inspect concrete pads for cracks.

Remove mildew.

If the decking is cedar, a spot of black slime may not be mildew; it could be a natural substance that sometimes leaches out. Just wash it with a mild soap-and-water solution. If you have other types of wood or if the black slime persists and seems related to moisture, then you've got mildew. It won't affect the strength of your wood, but you will want to get rid of it.

Use a commercial deck cleaner, or mix your own with a solution of one part chlorine bleach to three parts water. Use a stiff brush to work the solution into the wood. Rinse thoroughly with clean water and let the deck dry. This solution also can be effective in restoring some of the natural color to the deck. When you apply the next coat of finish to the deck, be sure it contains a mildewcide.

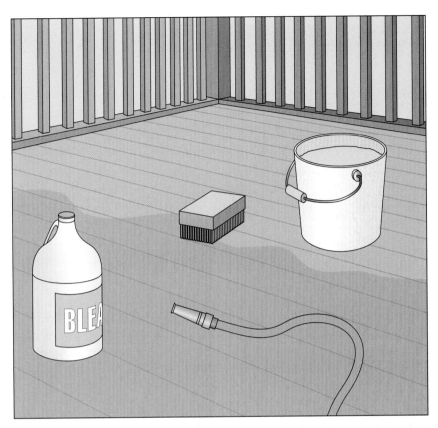

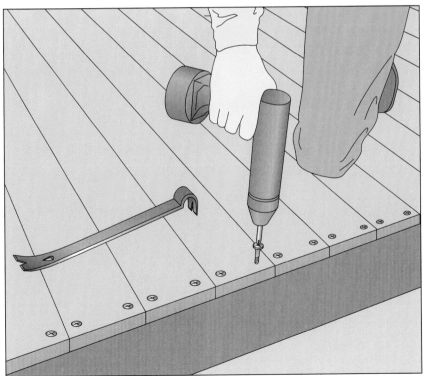

Replace popping nails.

As decking shrinks, nail heads may need to be hammered in farther. Over time, however, nails may start to loosen in their holes. In this case, carefully remove the nails, using a flat pry bar and/or a small piece of scrap wood to keep from denting the surface of the deck. Replace the nails with 3-inch decking screws. Or, drive new nails into the old holes in the decking, but at a different angle to avoid the old holes in the joists.

EXPERTS' INSIGHT

THE BENEFITS OF STAINLESS STEEL

Steel fasteners used on decks are coated, generally by galvanizing, to prevent the fasteners from corroding and staining the surrounding wood. Over time, however, most galvanized fasteners will begin to corrode. Double-coated and anodized decking screws are protected better than standard galvanized screws, but even they may lose their coatings over time. If you live in a particularly humid region or where the deck may be exposed to saltwater, the corrosion will begin sooner. In these latter cases, more expensive stainless steel fasteners may be a bargain in the long run because they won't corrode. They look great too.

GLOSSARY

For words not listed here, or for more about those that are, refer to the index, pages 110–112.

Actual dimension. The true size of a piece of lumber, after milling and drying. See *nominal dimension*.

Awl. A sharp-pointed tool used for making small starter holes for screws or for scribing lines.

Baluster. The small vertical members of a railing system, usually spaced at regular intervals between posts.

Beam. A large horizontal framing piece, usually made of 4× or doubled 2× lumber, which usually rests on posts and is used to support joists.

Bevel cut. An angle cut through the thickness of a piece of wood.

Blocking. Short pieces of lumber, usually the same dimension as the joists, cut to fit between joists. Blocking prevents the warping of joists and adds strength.

Board. A piece of lumber that is less than 2 inches thick and more than 3 inches wide.

Board foot. The standard unit of measurement for wood. One board foot is equal to a piece 12×12×1 inches (nominal size).

Building codes. Community ordinances governing the manner in which a home may be constructed or modified. Most codes deal primarily with fire and health concerns and have separate sections relating to electrical, plumbing, and structural work.

Butt joint. The joint formed by two pieces of material when fastened end to end, end to face, or end to edge.

Chamfer. A bevel cut made along the length of a board edge.

Cleat. A length of board attached so as to strengthen or add support to a structure.

Clinch. To hammer the exposed tip of a nail at an angle, bending its point into the surrounding wood for added joint strength.

Concrete. A building and paving material made by mixing water with sand, gravel, and cement. Deck posts typically rest on footings made of concrete.

Counterbore. A method of setting a screw so its head is below the surface of the surrounding wood. The void created is filled later with putty or plugged.

Countersink. To drive in the head of a nail or screw so its top is flush with the surface of the surrounding wood.

Crosscut. To saw a piece of lumber perpendicular to its length and/or its grain.

Decking. The boards used to make the walking surface of a deck. Decking is usually made of 2×4, 2×6, or ⁵/₄×6 lumber.

Edging. Pieces of wood used to cover the edges of boards.

Elevation drawing. A view of the deck that shows the vertical face.

End grain. The ends of wood fibers, which are exposed at the ends of boards.

Flashing. Strips of sheet metal, usually galvanized or aluminum, used to protect lumber from rain water. On a deck, flashing often is used to cover the ledger.

Flush. On the same plane, or level with, the surrounding surface.

Footing. A small foundation, usually made of concrete, used to support a post.

Frost heave. The upthrust of soil caused when moist soil freezes. Posts and footings that do not extend below the frostline are subject to frost heave.

Frostline. The maximum depth at which the ground in a particular region freezes during winter.

Furring. Lightweight strips of wood applied to surfaces to provide a plumb nailing surface for paneling or drywall.

Grain. The direction and pattern of fibers in a piece of wood.

Hardwood. Lumber that comes from leaved, deciduous trees, such as oak and maple.

Joist. Horizontal framing member that support a floor and/or ceiling.

Joist hanger. A metal connector used to join a joist to a ledger, beam, or rim joist so their top edges are flush.

Kerf. The void created by the blade of a saw as it cuts through a piece of material.

Lag screw. A screw, usually ¼ inch in diameter or larger, with a hexagonal head that can be driven with an adjustable or socket wrench.

Lap joint. The joint formed when one member overlaps another.

Lattice. A horizontal surface made of crisscrossed pieces of wood.

Ledger. A horizontal strip (typically lumber) used to provide support for the ends or edges of other members.

Level. The condition that exists when any type of surface is at true horizontal. Also a tool used to determine level.

Linear foot. The actual length of a board or piece of molding. See also *board foot*.

Miter joint. The joint formed when two members meet that have been cut at the same angle, usually 45 degrees.

Molding. A strip of wood, usually small-dimensioned, used to cover exposed edges or as decoration.

Nominal dimension. The stated size of a piece of lumber, such as a 2×4 or a 1×12. The actual dimension is somewhat smaller.

On-center (OC). A term used to designate the distance from the center of one regularly spaced framing member to the center of the next one.

Pier. A vertical piece of concrete, used as a footing to support a post. Make your own piers by pouring concrete, or purchase a ready-made concrete pier.

Pilot hole. A small hole drilled into a wooden member to avoid splitting the wood when driving in a screw or nail.

Plan drawing. An overhead view of a deck, which shows locations of footings and framing members.

Plumb. The condition that exists when a member is at true vertical.

Plywood. A building material made of sheets of wood veneer glued together with the grains at 90-degree angles to each other.

Post. A vertical framing piece, usually 4×4 or 6×6, used to support a beam or a joist.

Pressure-treated wood. Lumber and sheet goods impregnated with one of several solutions to make the wood impervious to moisture and weather.

Rabbet. A step-shaped cut made along the edge of a piece of wood, used to join boards tightly.

Rim joist. The outside joist, to which the majority of joists are attached at right angles.

Rip. To saw lumber or sheet goods parallel to its grain pattern.

Riser. A board attached to the vertical cut surface of a stair stringer to cover up the gap between treads and to provide additional tread support.

Rout. To shape edges or cut grooves using a router.

Sealer. A protective, usually clear, coating applied to wood or metal.

Setback. The minimum distance between a property line and any structure, as delimited by local building codes.

Setting nails. Driving the heads of nails slightly below the surface of the wood.

Shim. A thin strip or wedge of wood or other material used to full a gap between two adjoining components or to help establish level or plumb.

Site plan. A map showing the location of a new building project on a piece of property.

Skirt or skirting. Horizontal pieces of lumber installed around the perimeter of a deck to conceal the area below the decking. Skirting may be made of solid boards, either vertical or horizontal, or of lattice to allow for air movement.

Softwood. Lumber derived from evergreen conifers, such as pines, firs, cedars, or redwoods.

Span. The distance covered by a beam, joist, or decking board between supporting structures.

Square. The condition that exists when one surface is at a 90-degree angle to another. Also a tool used to determine square.

Stringer. A diagonal board used to support treads and risers on a stairway. Stringers usually are made of 2×12s.

Three-four-five method. An easy, mathematical way to check whether a large angle is square. Measure 3 feet along one side and 4 feet along the other; if the corner is square, the diagonal distance between those two points will equal 5 feet.

Toenail. To drive a nail at an angle, so as to hold together two pieces of material.

Tongue-and-groove. A joint made using boards that have a projecting tongue on one edge and a corresponding groove on the opposite edge.

Warp. Any of several lumber defects caused by uneven shrinkage of wood cells.

INDEX

METRIC CONVERSIONS

U.S. UNITS TO METRIC EQUIVALENTS			METRIC UNITS TO U.S. EQUIVALENTS		
To Convert From	Multiply By	To Get	To Convert From	Multiply By	To Get
Inches	25.4	Millimeters	Millimeters	0.0394	Inches
Inches	2.54	Centimeters	Centimeters	0.3937	Inches
Feet	30.48	Centimeters	Centimeters	0.0328	Feet
Feet	0.3048	Meters	Meters	3.2808	Feet
Yards	0.9144	Meters	Meters	1.0936	Yards
Miles	1.6093	Kilometers	Kilometers	0.6214	Miles
Square inches	6.4516	Square centimeters	Square centimeters	0.1550	Square inches
Square feet	0.0929	Square meters	Square meters	10.764	Square feet
Square yards	0.8361	Square meters	Square meters	1.1960	Square yards
Acres	0.4047	Hectares	Hectares	2.4711	Acres
Square miles	2.5899	Square kilometers	Square kilometers	0.3861	Square miles
Cubic inches	16.387	Cubic centimeters	Cubic centimeters	0.0610	Cubic inches
Cubic feet	0.0283	Cubic meters	Cubic meters	35.315	Cubic feet
Cubic feet	28.316	Liters	Liters	0.0353	Cubic feet
Cubic yards	0.7646	Cubic meters	Cubic meters	1.3079	Cubic yards
Cubic yards	764.55	Liters	Liters	0.0013	Cubic yards
Fluid ounces	29.574	Milliliters	Milliliters	0.0338	Fluid ounces
Quarts	0.9464	Liters	Liters	1.0567	Quarts
Gallons	3.7854	Liters	Liters	0.2642	Gallons
Drams	1.7718	Grams	Grams	0.5644	Drams
Ounces	28.350	Grams	Grams	0.0353	Ounces
Pounds	0.4536	Kilograms	Kilograms	2.2046	Pounds

To convert from degrees Fahrenheit (F) to degrees Celsius (C), first subtract 32, then multiply by ⅝.

To convert from degrees Celsius to degrees Fahrenheit, multiply by ⅝, then add 32.